JUST SHOOT IT!

A Complete Guide to Filmmaking From Script to Screen

2nd Edition

CURTIS KESSINGER

Copyright © 2012 Curtis Kessinger

All rights reserved. No part of this book may be used or reproduced in any manner whatsoever without written permission from the publisher, except in the case of brief quotations embodied in critical articles and reviews.

Published by Blue Heron Publications

Interior formatting by Kimberly Martin of Jera Publishing

Kessinger, Curtis
Just Shoot It!

Paperback Book
ISBN-10: 0-9777279-1-2
ISBN-13: 978-0-9777279-1-9

Contents

Acknowledgments 1
Introduction 3

1. Principles of Success 5
2. The Audience 9
3. Your Script 11
4. Phases of Production 33
5. Budgets, Contracts & Schedules 37
6. Casting 47
7. Production Design 49
8. Equipment 53
9. Insurance & Permits 55
10. Locations 57
11. Shooting Plan 59
12. Pacing 73
13. Directing 75

Cinematography

14. Camera Lenses 83
15. Lens Sizes 95

Composition

16. Camera Shots 103
17. Shooting Techniques 117
18. Camera Angles 123
19. Camera & Subject Movement 131
20. Balance 139
21. Center of Interest 143

Continuity

22. 180° Rule of Continuity 149
23. Lead Your Action 153
24. Overlap Your Action 155
25. Frame Entrances & Exits 157

Light

26. Types of Lighting 161
27. Basic Lighting Setup 163
28. Lighting Contrast 167
29. Lighting Placement 171
30. Lighting Choices 175
31. Power Requirements 177
32. Colors of Light 179

Sound

33. Sound 183

Post

34. Editing 191

Your Finished Film

35. The Business Side 205
36. The Golden Question 211

Conclusion 213
About the Author 215
Glossary 217
Additional Info and Resources 221

"No one else has the same passion
for your film that you do so
no one else is willing to sacrifice
what you are willing to sacrifice."

Acknowledgments

This book is dedicated to: my parents and siblings for allowing me to grow and develop into an independent, creative person; my wife and kids for showing me what's most important in life and for their constant support, especially in my writing and filmmaking endeavors; and friends, acquaintances and strangers for providing me with an infinite amount of material.

I wrote this book for one simple reason. I want to give filmmakers one book that tells them what they need to shoot their films. I want you to make your films. I want you to succeed so I can experience them with the rest of the audience. I have made my own films, financed and shot by me, with a small crew of volunteers, for little money...money that is within everyone's budget and I am always working on new films. I have worked on numerous films since 1990, asked a million questions, and written down everything I was told. All of the filmmaking knowledge I have gained I applied to this book. I appreciate everyone who has helped me and the names are too numerous to list. Now it's my turn to help you. If you will take the time to learn the skills in this book you will have what you need to make your films. If I can do it, then you can do it.

Special thanks to Anita Patterson Peppers, Clara Natoli, Phaedra Wilkinson, P. Winberg, Xenia Antunes, Luis Tejo, Scott Liddell, Ken Kiser, Sanjay Pindiyath and Keith Richardson for use of their great photos. Their work can be found on www.morguefile.com. I want to thank all of the corporate sponsors as well for use of their photos and for producing quality equipment that make this industry possible. Thank you!

Introduction

Welcome Filmmakers! Congratulations to you for taking the most important step to succeeding in the film business. You have decided to take matters into your own hands by learning how to make your own films. You can truly accomplish anything you want once you decide to do it! The motto of this book is simple. *Just Shoot It!* How much more simple can it get? *Just Shoot It!* was written to teach you everything you need to know to shoot your own films. It was written so that you know how to handle each job in case you don't have the money to hire people. Even if you have the money to hire people, you still need to know if they are performing their job to meet your expectations. The professional-level aspects of filmmaking are explained in simple terms so that you can understand them. If you will take the time to learn the creative, technical and business sides of filmmaking then you can be unstoppable. You can be in control of your film career. You will be dangerous to the film business. Dare to be dangerous.

Filmmaking has its own language and like learning any new language, repetition is the key to becoming fluent. Take the time to learn this language. It doesn't matter what type of films you are making: narrative, fiction, documentary, industrial, animation, experimental, training, TV, commercials, music videos, web series, etc., this film language applies to all of them. Learn it, then improvise and break the rules, but if you decide to break the rules, break them for a reason.

Filmmaking literally means making films. You have to shoot, shoot, shoot. The only training that works is on the job training. You learn by doing and by making mistakes. Your filmmaking skills will improve each and every day. The thought of making a film can be a scary and overwhelming undertaking, but once you start taking action and making films you will realize you can succeed. Did you take your driver's license test without ever having driven a car? Maybe you did, but most people would have failed their driving test without first practicing their driving skills. Practice your filmmaking skills.

There are several myths about the film industry. One is that success depends on who you know. Having connections helps, but it is not a requirement. You don't have to know anyone in the industry and I'm sure most of you don't. If you make a great film everyone will want to know you, so don't sit around and wait to meet the right people. Other common myths are that you can't make your own films without tons of money and without a professional cast and crew. None of these apply. People are out there making films with little money and without professional cast and crew. Don't wait for anyone to offer you anything, because nothing will be handed to you. It's time for you to make your own opportunities. If you make a great film your phone will ring off the hook and you will have the industry knocking down your door to work with you. You are in control of your own future. If you want your films to be made, you are going to have to make them yourself. No one can stop you from making great films. Everyone is one great film away from huge success. Filmmaking requires planning, effort, enthusiasm and time. Money is not the determining factor it once was. The financial barriers to filmmaking have been torn down so everyone walking the face of this earth can now make a film for very little money. Digital tools have allowed everyone to chase after their filmmaking dreams.

This book gives you the education and motivation you need to make your own films without having to spend a small fortune. It is designed so that you read a chapter, study and analyze films, and shoot footage using a basic camera. You can study and analyze films of your choice rather than films you may not like. Study films similar to the type or genre you want to shoot. It is also wise to study a variety of films in order to develop as much range as you possibly can. You don't need an expensive camera for the exercises. Get your hands on any camera. It doesn't have to be the camera you will ultimately use to shoot your films. Shooting is shooting. Filmmaking is filmmaking.

CHAPTER 1

Principles of Success

Success in the film industry is no different than success in any other industry. The principles of success are the same.

Belief

The first principle of success is belief. If you believe you can accomplish something then you can. If you don't believe it then you are guaranteed to fail. Success is 80-90% psychological. Will you have moments of doubt and disbelief? Of course you will, but you must keep marching onward. You will wake up in the middle of the night scared out of your wits, but keep believing. Believe you are a filmmaker. Believe it from this moment forward. You are no longer someone thinking and talking about making films. You are a filmmaker! Every person you see is a possible actor. Every building, every street and every park you see is now a possible shooting location. Why? You are a filmmaker that's why. Believe it! You have to believe it in your mind! If anyone asks you what you do for a living tell them you are a filmmaker. The more people you tell the more empowered you become. No actor in the world says they are a lawyer, waiter, or accountant, even if they are making their living as a lawyer, waiter or accountant. However you make your living, filmmaker is what you truly are so give yourself credit. Think and act like a filmmaker.

Focus

The ability to focus is another principle of success. You have to focus on the activities that will bring you the best results. Focus on the activities that will make your dreams come true. If you focus on the wrong activities then you will waste your energy and valuable time. You have to have discipline to stay focused on the activities that will bring you success. Put together a plan with schedules and stick to your plan. Make sure to always evaluate your progress and make sure your plan is the right plan. If it's not the right plan, then make changes. In order for you to be successful you have to move forward daily by setting daily goals, not weekly, monthly or yearly goals. Set daily goals/targets to meet or you will not make progress. Maybe each day you want to write 7-10 pages of script, storyboard 5 pages of script, cast your main character, find a cinematographer, shoot 2 pages of script, etc. At the end of each day check your progress and determine if you hit or missed your targets. Did you set them too high or too low? Did you waste time doing something else? How are you going to make up for the lost time to get back on track? Always ask yourself a few questions while looking in the mirror. Did you go all out and give it everything you had today? Could you have done more? What are you going to do tomorrow to move closer to success? Commit to being successful and hold yourself accountable. At the end of each day write down what you plan on accomplishing the next day. If you plan each day you know exactly what will happen that day. Learn to manage your time and eliminate all distractions. You are inventing your own future. No one else can control your future unless you allow it. You are in charge. You are your own CEO. You are the President of yourself. Only one person can stop you from succeeding and that person is you.

No Excuses

Successful people don't make up excuses. They keep moving forward. People love to make up excuses so they don't actually have to try and succeed. The two most-used excuses are a lack of money and a lack of time! Films can be professionally made for little money so that is not a valid excuse. Everyone has the same 24 hours in each day in which to accomplish his or her goals so this is also not a valid excuse. Some people accomplish a great deal while others accomplish absolutely nothing. If people spent as much time making films as they did coming up with excuses, they would have succeeded a long time ago. Realize there are no valid excuses, because filmmakers are out there succeeding! Either you are making films or making excuses! You can't do both.

Taking Action

Taking Action is another principle of success. If you take action towards making your films you can move ahead of the rest of the people who only talk about it. The difference between success and failure is simple...taking action. People who take action turn their dreams into reality. If you are not used to taking action then you will have to break out of those old habits and develop new ones. Don't try to do everything all at once. Take one step at a time. Learn to spend time on what you need to accomplish. It's too easy to sit and admire your past accomplishments. Keep yourself hungry so you continue to move forward. Keep driving to get better each and every day. Act with urgency by setting those daily goals. If you were to set weekly goals then you can waste several days each week without doing anything, because you have given yourself 7 days. Daily action means daily progress.

Handling Failure

Handling failure is an important principle of success. When you try anything new the usual outcome is failure. Most people stop trying after their first failure. Failure is simply telling you that you need more practice. If you learn from your failures then the word failure means education. Learn and move forward. Filmmaking is not difficult. It takes time and planning.

Handling Rejection

Handling rejection is another principle of success and might be the hardest to overcome. Most people are not comfortable with rejection. To be in the film industry or any part of the entertainment industry you have to listen to most people say "no" without you giving up. You have to keep going forward until you get the one person you need to say "yes." When someone says "no" it means you haven't given them a reason to say "yes." Don't take the rejection personally. In time you will realize being rejected is the norm.

Here is your success plan:
- Focus on the right activities
- Stay disciplined
- Make decisions - Indecision will stop you
- Plan your daily activities
- Take action each day
- At the end of the day determine your progress
- Revise your plan
- Never give up

If you don't shoot your films you will get old wondering if you could have done it. Can you deal with the thought that you came so close, but stopped short of trying? The pain and mental anguish of not trying will hurt more than actually giving it a shot. There are millions of people looking back on their lives wishing they had chased after their dreams. Don't be a member of that group. You have to do it! This is what you were meant to do.

CHAPTER 2

The Audience

As they say in the Business World, think like your customer. In the film business your customer is the audience. Films are made for the audience. In order for you to be a great filmmaker you also have to be a great audience member. If you are making your film just for you then you might be the only one watching it...in your living room. Your audience is going to give you their hard-earned money to see your film so they trust you to deliver what they want, but do you know what they want? The majority of the film-going audience wants to be moved emotionally by your film no matter the genre of your film. They have to be emotionally connected to your film. If you don't deliver what they want then the theater seats will be empty. You want the seats filled to capacity and an audience that is afraid to leave their seats out of fear of missing something.

Never underestimate your audience. Audiences are very smart so you don't have to point everything out to them. Let the audience think for themselves. Let them experience your film. Respect them. Engage them. Take them on a ride to a place where they have never been before. If the characters in your film want the same things in their film life as your audience wants in their real life then the audience can relate to them and root for them. Audiences want to see a film which shows them how to get what they want in their life: love, laughter, respect, security, fantasy, hope, resolution, justice, freedom, dreams coming true, etc. Few audience members want to see a film and experience what is happening in their everyday life and have the film turn out like their everyday life. They want hope that their own life will turn out better than it is at the present time. A great film can give your audience the motivation to take action to change their own life. You have them hooked by showing them a vision of their own future.

Great filmmakers are masters at getting the audience to feel whatever it is they want them to feel. They do this by using the script, acting, cinematography, set design, lighting, editing, etc. This book teaches you how to do the same, but first you must determine what you want the audience to feel at any given moment such as shock, love, hate, anger, empathy, uneasy laughter, wet-their-pants hysterical laughter, loathing, sympathy, fear, surprise, inspiration, powerful, enlightened, nervous, etc. Determine what you want them to feel. Weave as many emotions into your film as possible. You don't want one emotion running through your entire film. Take them on a roller coaster ride of emotions.

The audience doesn't understand all the hard work that went into making your film. They don't notice the camera, lighting, sound and production design, etc. All they see is the end product...the sum of all the parts. The audience does notice when things are wrong. The audience knows the truth when they see it, feel it and hear it, so don't try and fool them. They will know.

The reason you make your film for the audience is so it has a chance of being distributed to as many outlets as possible. The film business is a business. You want the chance to continue to make films.

The audience is waiting for great films to arrive. Give them what they want.

CHAPTER 3

Your Script

Your goal is to make a great film by telling a great story! Great films don't come from good scripts, they come from great scripts. Challenge yourself to write great scripts. One of the main reasons most films fail is that they start production with a bad or good script instead of a great script. Don't follow in those footsteps. Focus your time on your script until it is great.

What do you know about screenwriting? Maybe you know everything or maybe you don't know anything. If your plan is to sell your script or film to investors or to the Hollywood players, then you need to understand what they normally look for in a script/film. You also have to develop an interest in your script from your possible cast and crew. Your audience also has certain expectations.

Most everyone expects original, classic storytelling, which dates back thousands of years. Structure is simply how everything is arranged in your script. This structure has a Beginning, Middle and End or Act I, Act II and Act III as the sections are more often called. Some writers like to break the script up into four parts or eight parts, but the three-act structure is the basic starting point. The Beginning section (Act I) is approximately 25% of your story, the Middle section (Act II) is approximately 50% and the End section (Act III) is approximately 25%. These are rough approximations and are meant as a guide not as a strict rule.

Can you break the rules? Yes! Break the rules by developing original stories. Go for it but also know the risks involved.

Classic Storytelling Structure

Beginning – Act I - 25%

Start off by setting up your story: the who, what, when, and where of your story. You want to show/introduce your Main Character first since the audience identifies most with the first person they see on the screen. Other characters may be seen first, but the real center of attention at the start of your story should be your Main Character. For purposes of this book the term Main Character represents female, male and multiple main characters. The Main Character is also known as the protagonist, hero, or good guy/gal. In *The Wizard of Oz* Dorothy is the first person seen and the center of attention. In *Jaws* Police Chief Brody is not the first person seen, but he is the center of attention at the start. In *The King's Speech* you see Bertie about to make a speech and you instantly know his problem. In *Saturday Night Fever* you know everything about John Travolta's character Tony before the opening credits are done rolling. It is one of the best film openings ever for setting up the Main Character. The scene shows Tony walking down the sidewalk carrying a can of paint in step with the music. That's as simple as you can get? But oh, how revealing it is!

Films usually start off with the Main Character in their current situation. This situation may or may not be a positive, everything-is-all-right situation. Usually things in their life are normal and in-balance or at least things appear to be normal and in-balance. It's a so-called perfect world. Their life may be a complete wreck, but for them that is normal. Most often things are not as they appear.

The Big Bang

Then Bang, something happens. The problem has arrived, which is usually caused by the opposition. The opposition is also known as the antagonist, villain, rival, anti-hero, bad guy/gal, rival, foe, or adversary. The opposition doesn't have to be another person. It could be an animal

(*Jaws*), nature (*Twister, Perfect Storm*), etc. Inner opposition is always a part of every great script. This means the Main Character has internal issues/conflicts that prevent them from having the great life they deserve. Let's face it, everyone has issues. This Big Bang or problem is often called the **inciting incident** and it happens very early in the story. Now the story is set into motion. This is the spark that starts the fire. Everyday life has changed, because things are no longer the way they were. The status quo no longer exists. The so-called perfect world of the Main Character is now out-of-balance. It has become a new world, because that inciting incident changed their world in some way...good or bad. The new world is not necessarily a new place. It simply means things have changed in the place where the story first started. In *Jaws* the incident was the shark killing the girl at the start of the film. In *Finding Nemo* all the eggs are eaten except one...Nemo. In *Million Dollar Baby* the incident is when the girl boxer shows up to the gym. This changes everything at that gym. In *The Wizard of Oz*, the first shot of the film is Dorothy running, with Toto, down the dirt lane to their farm. This first image shows us things have already happened to set the story into motion. She is running from Miss Gulch, because Miss Gulch wants to take Toto away from her. In *The King's Speech* Bertie stammers during his speech so in a way it is the incident, but then Elizabeth goes to visit Lionel in regards to helping Bertie with his stammer. This starts a sequence of events leading up to Bertie visiting Lionel as well and Lionel making the recording of Bertie's voice.

    The incident doesn't have to be a murder, explosion or anything big. It could be something as simple as an arriving postcard, phone call or a visit from a friend. It is essentially a bug in the soup. If you can make the problem something relevant to the audience then they will be much more involved in your film. Speak to your audience. This incident has to be something that the Main Character has never been through before. It takes the Main Character and other characters out of their comfort zone. They wish they could make things go back the way they were, but it is too late. Things have changed and it will change them. They will learn new things about themselves and develop new insight and skills in order to try and get their lives back in order. The incident delivers the ultimate question to the audience: will the Main Character achieve their goal? Will he catch the killer, get the girl, save the town from death and destruction, save himself, get a new job after being fired, become rich and famous, learn to give a speech without stammering? Will Dorothy get back to Kansas? Will the Main Character's actions resolve the problem/fix the issue?

Up to this point in your story the Main Character hasn't committed to taking on the problem. They survey the changes/problem and wonder what has just happened. The Main Character is the one who has to face the problem and go after it, but at first there is reluctance to get involved. The Main Character may even run and hide. Bertie wanted nothing to do with Lionel and his strange ways of working. Dorothy ran away from home. As everyone can attest running away never works, because the problems always follow you. The only way to solve problems is to face them head-on.

The Bigger Bang

By the end of Act I a **Bigger Bang** happens…something much larger than the inciting incident! This may also be a series of events instead of one event that creates this bigger bang. The story moves forward in a new and different direction. It forces the Main Character to take action to resolve things…to try and set things straight…to fix what's broken or changed. They will have to commit to resolving the initial problem that was created by the incident and by the end of the Act I they have decided to commit to chasing the goal. This is the **Plot** of the film. This is the outer goal. In *Jaws* it's to catch/kill the shark. In *Finding Nemo*, Nemo is off to his first day of school which leads to him getting caught by the scuba divers. The goal is for Nemo to survive and for his dad to find him. In *Million Dollar Baby* it's to train the girl boxer. In *Walk the Line* Johnny Cash wanted to play music for a living. In *It's a Wonderful Life* it's to take over the savings and loan building so it doesn't close down. In *The Wizard of Oz*, it's to run away so Miss Gulch can't take Toto away, then a tornado hits which leads Dorothy into Oz and her quest to get back home. For Dorothy the plot is to get back home. In *The King's Speech* Bertie has to rid himself of his stammer if he is to become the leader of his nation in their time of need. He realizes Lionel proved to him that he could speak without stammering and now he decides to work with Lionel.

It's a big decision to go after the goal and the Main Character is confident. At first they think it will be a piece of cake, no problem solving this problem, but they are in for the shock of their life, because it is going to be extremely difficult to solve the problem. Chief Brody simply gathered up the local fishermen and had them hunt down the shark for him. Easy. Dorothy thought all she had to do was follow the yellow brick road and she would be able to get back home. It looked easy, but little did she know what was around the next corner.

So the Main Character decides to accept the challenge of going after the problem and off they go on the adventure into Act II. You must realize that all the characters in your film should have goals and take actions to accomplish them. They too will be in for the ride of their life.

Middle – Act II - 50%

Now the Main Character enters into the new world! This is where the real journey and life lessons begin. This new uncharted territory has new rules and the Main Character must learn these rules in order to survive and be successful in accomplishing their goal (plot). The audience learns almost everything about our Main Character, both personally and professionally. They see what the Main Character is made of. Are they made of steel or glass? Brave or cowardly? Emotionally strong or weak? The characters will reveal themselves to the audience. Their actions show everyone who they truly are.

Act II is the real story...the drama...the conflict...the tension...the emotion. Even in comedies you must have drama, conflict, tension and emotion. The drama increases every step of the way. The conflict increases. The tension increases. The emotions increase. The obstacles increase. The risks increase. The Main Character must take bigger and bigger actions to achieve the goal. The closer they get to the goal the further away it seems and the more dangerous it gets, because everybody wants the same goal, but not everybody can have it. The Main Character and the opposition fight harder and harder for the goal.

In *Walk the Line* Johnny Cash hits the road to make a living playing his music. It takes him away from his wife and family. It is new territory for him.

In *The Wizard of Oz* Dorothy has literally landed in this new colorful world. She has a rough road ahead of her and she must learn how to survive in it or she will not reach her goal. Has there ever been a more opposing force than the Witch? A cute little farm girl versus a Wicked Witch! Talk about opposites.

Remember Jack Nicholson in *One Flew Over the Cuckoo's Nest*? He thought that going to the mental ward would be better than going to prison. But little did he realize who he was dealing with. His opposition Nurse Ratched was one tough cookie. He and Nurse Ratched were complete opposites. Both of them wanted control of the mental ward. Jack wanted it his way which opposed Nurse Ratched's way. Jack was the loud, boisterous, fun-loving rebel and she was cold, calculated and quiet. She was a nasty villain. The villain doesn't have to be big, loud and unruly. It's the opposite ones that get under the audience's skin...all the way to the bone. She was wicked.

In *The Lord of the Rings* Frodo had to leave his beautiful world to enter into this forbidden, dangerous world. He was this small, peaceful person and his opposition was beyond wicked and horrible.

In *The King's Speech* Bertie takes over the throne and he must deliver to his people. The pressure mounts.

Point of No Return

By the halfway point of Act II the Main Character realizes this is not as easy as was first thought. They think they can still win this battle, but it's getting tougher every step of the way. They have swum halfway across the lake and there is no use in going back now. They must go forward. There is just enough gas in the car to go forward or back, but going back will not solve the inevitable problem, so the only way to go is forward. It is a difficult decision, because once they choose to go forward they cannot go back. But it is the right choice. The problem can be solved with more effort. At this point the Main Character is no longer the same person they were at the beginning of this story. They have developed new skills, learned a few things, grown and reached a point in the journey where they know they cannot go back. This is called the **Point of No Return**. They fully commit to the goal now. They are all in and going for the win! They are going to have to make bigger decisions and take riskier actions. Everything escalates. The pace of the story quickens. Fasten your seatbelts folks it's going to be a bumpy ride.

At Death's Door

From the halfway point in Act II up to the end of Act II things get much worse. At the end of Act II your Main Character has reached their lowest point in the film. Your Main Character has reached the bottom of the pit. All seems lost. Game over! It's hopeless now. The chances of resolving things are somewhere between slim and none. The Main Character is mentally and physically gone. Things cannot get worse. This is the end of trying to solve the goal. Death has arrived! The Main Character has caused all of this to happen. Their actions have led them to the bottom of the pit. Will they accept death or reach down deep and overcome this greatest obstacle? How on earth will they make it one more step? They are as far away from the goal as they have ever been. How can this be? Everything possible has been done to make it work and it has led them to this point...the lowest point possible.

In *The Wizard of Oz*, Dorothy will be killed by the witch and won't make it back to Kansas.

In *It's a Wonderful Life*, George is ready to commit suicide, because he feels his life is worthless.

In *Jaws*, Police Chief Brody is about to be eaten by the shark.

In *The Lord of the Rings* Frodo will be killed and the ring will be back in the hands of the Dark Lord Sauron.

In *Walk the Line* Johnny Cash was at the end of his rope. Addicted to drugs and alcohol he felt his life was no good to anyone. All he had done was hurt people. He felt worthless. He had a choice...give up or get cleaned up.

In *The King's Speech* Bertie finds out Lionel has no credentials...no diploma...no training...he is not a doctor...he is a fraud. Bertie had vouched for Lionel and it is now backfiring. Bertie has now lost every ounce of confidence he had gained by working with Lionel. The nation has a voiceless King for a leader. His family has lost confidence in him. He is about to make a speech that may determine the future of his country and empire. War is looming overhead. To top it all off if he fails his brother David could take over the throne. The people he is supposed to lead are not on his side. They do not believe a stammering King can lead them in these times of need. They have heard him speak before and they are not behind him. Here is a man with no friends, a deserting populace and even his own family fears the worst for him.

In every *romantic comedy film*, the couple has no chance of finding love. No getting back together.

So now our Main Character is close to death. The biggest obstacle to overcome has arrived. Will the Main Character come back from the dead?

End – Act III - 25%

Here we go! The final countdown to the final showdown! The big confrontation. The mother of all battles! The main event! It all comes together. The emotions, the strategy, the plan, the help, the hard work, the gained knowledge…all must be put to good use to win.

The Climax

The Main Character must figure out how to avoid death…figure out how to get off the bottom. Everything has been tried and it didn't work. The one place yet to be explored is inward. Deep inside there is inner conflict. Maybe something has been missing in their quest. The inner need is missing. This is discovered in the **Subplot**. Up to this point their inner goal has been ignored. The audience realized the Main Character had this need, but they didn't realize it until now. It's like drug addicts finally realizing they have a problem. The Main Character realizes they have been chasing the wrong goal. They have been chasing the outer goal instead of the inner goal. Wow! The Main Character must solve the inner conflict (the subplot) before they can solve the outer conflict (the plot). Now they realize they must change in order to solve the problem. Shear guts and action won't do it. They have to get personal and understand that this weakness has been keeping them from success. They must grow personally in order to solve the plot.

What is going to happen? The Main Character struggles to breathe...struggles to their knees...wobbles to their feet and just when it looked like sure death they get stronger and stronger. They rise up and conquer the inner and outer goals...they solve both problems...solve both conflicts. They have completed the tasks, solved the problems and gone through their transformation...their **character arc**.

In *The Wizard of Oz*, Dorothy realizes there is no place like home. She knows her real goal is the inner need to be home. For her there is no better place than home.

In *It's a Wonderful Life*, George realizes his life impacted many people and saved many lives. He knows he is rich in terms of friends not money. Money does not make you wealthy...friends do.

In *Jaws*, Police Chief Brody overcomes his fear of water and takes control of the situation to get the shark.

In *Walk the Line* Johnny Cash has to overcome his addictions and his past relationship with his father. He never felt he was good enough for his father.

In *The King's Speech* Bertie realizes that Lionel has taught him to stand up for himself. Taught him to have a voice that he never had before. Lionel has actually become the only friend he has ever had. He has become King and now must make the most important speech in the history of the empire. He must show them they have a leader they can trust and he does. He does with flying colors.

Resolution

In the end things need to be resolved. If you set something up in the story then resolve it so the audience gets closure. Don't leave them hanging. Nothing else is left to finish up. Everyone lives happily ever after or gets what they deserved. In *The Wrestler* Randy "The Ram" Robinson died doing what he loved...performing for the crowd. *No Country For Old Men* left the audience hanging, because the bad guy Chigurh murdered innocent people and got away with it. The majority of the audience didn't like that ending. Did we ever know where the chicken came from in *The*

Hangover? That was a very minor issue, but the ticket-buying audience likes to have things wrapped up and they like to leave knowing everything they needed to know. If things are wrapped up the audience goes out into the real world and solves their own personal problems, and helps others to solve their problems. You have changed the world by making such a great film.

Now that the classic story structure has been laid out...let's take a more detailed look at key script elements.

Logic

Your script/film must make sense. Things must happen for a reason and the audience must see things as being logical for the world in which your film takes place. Flying monkeys in *The Wizard of Oz* seemed logical for all the other things the audience had seen up to that point. *Star Wars* sets up the future world in which the film took place and everything including the wild, unique characters seemed logical. Throwing random events into a film for no reason other than a way to fix things isn't logical. Sure, in real life strange coincidences happen, but this is not real life...this is **reel** life. This is a film and it better make sense to the audience. The best reason for something to happen is that one of the characters causes it to happen by their actions. Don't pull a rabbit out of your hat. Use logic. Ask yourself, "would this actually happen and did this happen because one of the characters caused it to happen?"

Plot

This is what the audience thinks the film is about. Plot is the action of the story...the stuff on the surface that drives the story. The Main Character's goal or want, is the thing they knowingly chase after. It is the plot. This is where the main problem has to be solved. Plot must come from the choices the characters make and the actions they take to solve their problems. Those actions must drive the plot and determine where the story goes, not the other way around. Don't try and force characters into a plot or they will be superficial characters and forced to act a certain way to fit the plot. Let their emotional action drive the story. Characters make decisions and take actions to solve problems and they come up short. What the Main Character expects to happen and what actually does happen are two different things. Their efforts fall short time after time and they must regroup and take new steps each time to try and solve the problem. The same goes for the other characters. They often feel they are going backwards but they must continue to take new directions to try and solve the problem. The complications increase each time until the final climactic point in the film when they actually solve the problem and the other characters solve their problems.

Will they get the goal in the end? It all depends on what it is. If it is a meaningful goal then the answer is usually yes. If it is about superficial, materialistic things like wealth, power, sex, etc., then they may not achieve their goal. And rightly so, because they usually get what they need not what they want.

In *Finding Nemo*, Nemo's father was trying to find his son...a meaningful goal.

Al Pacino in *Scarface* was chasing money through crime...not a meaningful goal.

In *The King's Speech* Bertie was trying to speak without stammering and lead his people...a meaningful goal.

Subplot

This is the real story. Great films have many subplots. The theme is carried in the subplot. A great script is really about the Main Character and their underlying story which is their need. The Main Character gets what they need, without really knowing they had the need throughout the story. The need/goal in the subplot is more important to the Main Character than the want/goal in the plot. Their need usually centers on love, family, friendship, hope, security, justice, respect, values and morals, things that cannot be bought. This is where real life enters into the story. Keep real life happening and you can keep your audience involved. Give the audience something to think about while the film is unfolding.

In *Walk the Line* Johnny Cash has several subplots: his love for June Carter, overcoming his addictions, and his past relationship with his father.

In *Field of Dreams*, another past relationship with a father is at stake.

In *Rocky*, Rocky received love from Adrian and earned respect for his fight even though he lost the championship.

Most of the film's emotions reside in the subplot. Don't let your audience ride along on one emotion the whole time. There must be victory and defeat along the journey. Keep the emotional roller coaster ride going. Let your audience laugh and cry. This is where the Main Character can grow and change by solving the emotional problem in the subplot.

For the Main Character to solve the plot they must first solve the subplot. Chasing after the plot impacts the subplot and visa-versa. This conflict adds another dimension to the script. Solving one risks solving the other.

Summary of Plot and Subplot

Plot	Subplot
External Story	Internal Story
Action	Emotion Driven Action
Outer Goal	Inner Goal
Want	Need
Muscle	Brains/Heart
The Fight	The Love

Great films have a plot and several subplots. Of course these subplots could actually be plots for other characters besides the Main Character.

In *Jaws* the plot was to catch/kill the shark, but in order to do that Police Chief Brody had to overcome his fear of the water. Catch the shark (outer goal) and overcome fears/flaws/weakness (inner goal). Police Chief Brody risks his life and his family's well being to help others. If he were to stay with his family then he risks more danger to swimmers by not catching/killing the shark, having to shut down the beach, chasing away the tourists and risking the financial death of the town. He also had the guilt of the boy who died because he didn't shut down the beach earlier. Either choice has risks and problems associated with that choice.

In *Scarface* the plot was to get rich and everything that comes with it. The subplot was to get married, raise a family, and take care of his mother, sister and best friend. The plot and subplot were in conflict with each other.

In *Walk the Line* Johnny Cash wanted to make his living playing his music and provide for his wife and children. But he was in love with another person...June. He was in love with her the second he saw her. The plot and subplot caused conflict, because as he was making his living out on the road with June, he couldn't resist her and it conflicted with his marriage and family life. His addictions were in conflict with his plot and subplots, because they threatened his very existence.

In *It's a Wonderful Life* the plot was for George to go to college, travel the world and build great things. This conflicted with the subplot of doing the right thing and taking over the Savings and Loan...thinking of others...putting them first. The plot and subplot were in conflict. By taking over the Savings and Loan, George would never have the money to travel the world or to see and build great things. George became rich with friends, support and love, which is more important than money. George got what he needed, which was to realize he had impacted many people's lives. He built great things by helping the townspeople own their own homes. He realized he had lived a wonderful life and his life was worth more than he could ever have imagined.

In *Witness* the plot was to catch a killer and possibly even kill them. One of the subplots was the romance with the Amish woman, which meant living a peaceful, non-violent life. The plot and subplot were in conflict. Working and living in a violent world was in conflict with the Amish way of life.

In *Field of Dreams* the plot was to save the farm before the bank foreclosed on it. The subplot was to have a second chance to play catch with his father...a second chance to show him how much he loved him. In order to be able to play catch with his father he had to plow under a large portion of his cornfield to build the baseball field, which caused him to lose money from the crops he destroyed. So the plot and subplot were in conflict. He had to choose one or the other and he chose the more risky move, which was plowing under the corn. He chose the subplot over the plot because it was more important. In the end he succeeded in achieving both goals. He was able to be with his father again and save the farm.

In *The King's Speech*, Bertie wanted to be able to lead his people, but he had to overcome his flaws and his stammer. He had to learn to be confident and stand up for himself and understand that he was worth listening to. He had always been marginalized for his stammer and for being the younger brother. He had to learn to be a friend and to have a friend. He had never had a friend in his whole life. He learned how to be a human being not just royalty.

What does the Main Character want and need? The Main Character is aware of the want, but not usually aware of the need. The audience is aware of the Main Character's need, but the Main Character isn't aware until late in the story. In the end the Main Character gets the need/inner goal, but may not get the want/outer goal. It takes overcoming their fears, flaws, weaknesses, etc. to get the need and the want....to solve the internal and external problems. The internal need must be solved for them to have a great life...a fulfilling life...a worthy life. The opposition keeps the Main Character from getting the outer goal and the Main Character is their own worst enemy when it comes to their inner goal. The two goals have to be intertwined. To get one goal requires getting the other. One may lead to the other. The inner need means having a need to change and grow, because something is missing from their life.

Theme

Theme is the message being told in a story. A story can have many themes. This is the moral part of the story...the moral way of life...the moral element of how people should live their life...the way things should be done. Weave the theme into the story, especially in the subplot or subplots. Bring out the theme slowly. Don't preach to the audience or try and cram the theme down their throat. Who is supporting the theme and who is against it? The opposition is an obstacle to the theme. The supporting cast may be on either side or they may waver back and forth between both sides. The Main Character may even waver back and forth in regards to the theme. Themes involving money versus family and friends are great moral conflicts. It's so true to life. Everyone struggles with wanting more money, but is it more important than family? No! The theme wins out in the end of the film, but not until the bottom of the 9th inning. All looked lost until the end.

It's a Wonderful Life used themes that family and friends are more important than money and that every one of us is capable of impacting many lives without us even knowing it. Underdogs and nice people can finish first. None of these themes looked like they were going to happen until the end of the film when the townspeople showed up to save George and the Savings and Loan. George had helped all of them and now it was their turn to pay him back.

Scarface used themes relating to overcoming your obstacles, having integrity, family over money, and that crime does not pay. The bad guys lose in the end. Most audiences want to see criminals get their due. It looked like the theme of crime doesn't pay was going to lose out up until the end of the film.

In *The Wizard of Oz*, it looked like Dorothy would not make it back home and the theme that family is most important would lose out. But in the end the theme won.

In *Walk the Line* several themes were involved. You can't stop love. You can get a second chance in life. Drugs and alcohol will ruin you and those around you.

In *Witness* peace won over violence. The theme won in the end of the film.

Lord of the Rings used a theme of good versus evil. Until the end of the film it looked like evil would win.

Field of Dreams used the theme of getting second chances in life and most of the characters in the film got a second chance in life.

In *Gladiator* themes of family, justice, democracy and honor were used and in the end of the film those proved to be true.

In *The King's Speech* it looked like Bertie would fail in his most important speech and let his family and people down. But it was his family and his friendship with Lionel that proved to be his ace card. They believed in him and helped him believe in himself.

Action

Films must be about your characters taking action and those actions are based on their emotions. Characters show their feelings by what they do or don't do. Doing nothing is also an action. Show the emotions of the characters. Instead of having Carlos say he's angry, have Carlos punch the wall or do something as simple as grinding his teeth. Remember, for every action there is a reaction, and then another reaction and on and on until the end. Taking action doesn't have to mean breaking down doors, shooting people, and chasing the villain. Taking action may mean getting out of bed earlier and showing up on time. Those seem like simple things, but they are action none-the-less.

Some people thought the Main Character in *The Pianist* was too passive by not taking action against the Nazis. Taking direct action against them would have meant sure death. The only action possible was to evade them, which he did. Survival was the action! In the end he took the action that saved his life by playing the piano for the Nazi soldier.

Conflict

Conflict makes a film interesting. Conflict is drama. Your Main Character must have opposition, road blocks, stumbles and struggles working against them as they pursue the goal. The conflict can come from nature, from within (their inner demons), from others, from society, from the law, etc. The inner conflict is most important. Everyone is flawed, because it is nearly impossible for anyone to look objectively at themselves and see their own problems. In the end the Main Character must overcome their internal problem in order to solve their main problem in the plot.

Character Arc

The arc is the personal change/growth any character goes through in the course of the film. This growth does not come easy. Not all characters will change/grow but those that do will go through hell and back to conquer their problems. The audience must see the characters wrestling with their problems and clawing their way past them. By the end of the film they have realized their inner conflict and overcome it. They have learned of their need and have found it. The arc changes the characters for the better. This is one main reason why people like to go to the movies. They witness people with problems like their own, but yet the movie characters solve their problems. It gives the audience hope for solving their own problems.

Characters

The audience experiences the film through the Main Character as they pursue their goal, but in order to keep the audience interested all characters have to be 3-dimensional. The audience has to experience the real emotions of the characters.

Tony in *Scarface* is a great example. On the surface the audience saw a ruthless and violent drug dealer who would do anything to get rich. Underneath was a man who had a sense of humor, wanted to get married and have a family, and cared about his mother, sister and best friend.

To develop great characters you have to get below the surface to reveal who they are underneath. The true person is always lurking just below the surface. Show the audience what's on the inside. Put them under the microscope...shine a light on them and apply some pressure and reveal the real inner character. Their personalities will come out. Their emotions will show up and drive their decision-making. If you don't know what your characters are feeling then ask them. Act like you are a therapist and get inside your characters. What are they thinking and what are they feeling? Characters make decisions based on their emotional reaction to what has happened. Every action they take must come from their emotions. They may say one thing, but what they do is what counts. Characters often say they are telling the truth when in fact they are not telling the truth. Tough guys never talk about being tough, they are tough. The guys that talk tough are scared out of their wits. Every horror film has one character who says, "Don't worry, I'm not afraid," but as soon as the horror arrives they are the most afraid. How characters react under pressure shows their true self.

Your Main Character has to be active. Active characters are much more interesting than passive ones. The audience wants to see characters take action to pursue their goals. They can't let everything happen to them. There is no reward for someone who won't risk everything to get what they want. The more risk the better. They have to make tough, life-threatening decisions. All decisions have to have consequences. Having to make a decision between good and evil can be easy, but deciding between two good choices or two evil choices is not easy and is more interesting. Having to make a decision that will cause problems either way is a tough decision, especially knowing that one choice causes them to permanently lose the other choice. Many of the problems that develop throughout the film are a direct result of the Main Character's decisions and actions. Reveal the story structure, plot, subplot, theme, etc. through the Main Character's decisions and actions.

The audience must identify with the Main Character and relate to their struggles in some way in order to stay interested. Empathy and sympathy are the ways people relate to the Main Character, because they see themselves or someone they know in the Main Character and feel for them as well. Characters can't be 100% good or 100% bad. Make them human by giving them problems, flaws, weaknesses and emotions. Show the audience the emotional side of your superheroes and villains. Some people would say it's hard to identify or relate to a criminal Main Character, but there is a side of the audience that roots for them, especially if the Main Character has no other choice and is trying to improve themselves.

Was Tony a likeable character in *Scarface*? For some people he was. Here was a man struggling to make it in a new country. Many audience members were able to relate to a character who was trying to improve his life and live the American Dream even though it was through criminal endeavors. He knew no other way of life. He showed his good side by trying to help and protect his mother and sister as they too struggled in a foreign land, but once he bettered himself he should have turned against a life of crime. Since he didn't he got what he deserved. And he destroyed the people he was trying to protect: his best friend, sister and mother. Everybody should get exactly what they deserve...good or bad.

Bonnie and Clyde were not upstanding, moral citizens and they got what they deserved.

Tom Hanks in *Road to Perdition* played a criminal and got what he deserved, but he taught his son to stay away from that lifestyle.

Create original 3-dimensional characters. The audience rarely sees original characters? How well do you know your characters? No two people have the same goals, needs, thoughts, etc. Your characters all have to stand out against everyone else in the story. Do you know their **Back Story**? This is their history. Everything that has happened in their life...everything that has made them who they are and the way they are, all happened in the back story before your script starts.

Do you know their:

Age, Height, Weight, Physical Appearance, Background, Education, Strengths, Weaknesses, Flaws, Fears, Work History, Military History, Family History, Sexual History, Beliefs (Religious, Political, Philosophical), Interests, Hobbies, Habits, Attitude, Sense of Humor, Secrets, Quirks, etc. Do they like to drink, smoke, or do drugs? How do they walk and talk? Who are their friends and enemies? Are they neat, sloppy, obsessive? How do they react under pressure? Many questions should be answered about your characters.

Dialog

Remember, film is a visual medium so show the audience something rather than telling them. Don't explain things using dialog. When a character doesn't say something it can be more powerful than when they do say something. Foreign films are better at using visuals than American films. Watch a few foreign films and notice how much simpler they seem, but they are actually more complex because they use visuals instead of dialog to get their message across. Use your dialog wisely. Say as much as you can with the least amount of words.

Dialog is not normal dialog. Film dialog is a representation of real dialog. You are compressing a story into two hours so every word has to count. Dialog has to be unique for each character. No two people talk alike. Characters rarely talk in full sentences. What characters say and do are often two different things. Characters say one thing, but often mean and do something else. They rarely say what they mean.

Most people think dialog is the best way to deliver the action, message or emotion of a scene, but in fact it is the worst. Find the best way to use visuals to deliver meaning to your audience.

Action Description

If you want to sell your script or garner interest from actors, investors, producers, etc., then make sure your script reads well. Everyone focuses on dialog and forgets the scene action. State the action in present tense as if it is happening now. Keep your reader interested by presenting an interesting and visual story. Describe it visually. Give your reading audience a picture of what is happening.

Characteristics of Great Scripts

- Great scripts have an outer goal/want and an inner goal/need that conflict with each other.
- Great scripts allow them to achieve both goals...the want and the need
- Great scripts have huge risks for the characters. Love, life and death are huge risks.
- Great scripts increase the stakes for more and more people as the script progresses.
- Great scripts have a Main Character with flaws, fears and weaknesses which allow the audience to become emotionally attached to them.
- Great scripts have all characters battling their own problems and goals.
- Great scripts have the opposition wanting the same thing that the Main Character wants.
- Great scripts are a representation of life, not life itself. Normal life is too boring, so skip the boring parts. If a camera crew followed you for a day, from the time you woke up, ate breakfast, and showered, etc., would the audience be on the edge of their seats? Not likely. One hour goes by and nothing interesting has happened. If you were to drive across the country it would take you days (real time), but in a film you only have a few hours of screen

YOUR SCRIPT 31

time (reel time). Films jump around, back and forth in time and space to eliminate those parts.
- Great scripts stay one step ahead of the audience. The audience is always looking/thinking ahead trying to figure out what is going to happen. Keep your audience off guard by staying one step ahead of them and keeping them guessing at what will come next. Baseball/softball pitchers keep the batter guessing by changing pitches. Just when the batter is expecting a fastball the pitcher throws them a curveball. Mix things up. Throw the audience curveballs. Get them to expect something and then give them something different. This creates tension and drama. Capture their attention and keep the momentum building all the way to the end.
- Great scripts have conflict coming from several different sources as well as internal conflict within the Main Character.
- Great scripts are logical.
- Great scripts get to the point of each scene. What is the one thing you are trying to achieve before you move on to the next scene? Each scene has to push the story forward. Why is each scene there? Can you get rid of any scenes and nothing will change? Any scene that doesn't add to the story needs to be removed. It's hard to part ways with some of your favorite characters and scenes, but you have to do it. Each scene needs to provide the audience with new information, new action, introduce us to new characters, set tempo and mood, etc. Know your goals for each scene.

Exercise: *Take your script and try and replace your dialog with actions that show us a character's true self. Work through all of your action description and replace it with interesting visual references. Make your script interesting to read.*

Are you 100% sure your script is ready to shoot? Does your cast and crew agree it's ready to shoot? Resolve all issues with your cast and crew prior to arriving on the set. Listen to their input. Put your ego in check and listen to everyone's input. Right or wrong their input can only help.

Script Reading

Have a script reading and record it so you can sit and listen to it afterwards to hear how your dialog sounds.

Copyright

Register your treatment, script and film with the US Copyright Office to protect you in case of a copyright infringement. The Writers Guild registration does not offer you the same protection as a copyright in a court of law. Contact the US Copyright Office or go to their website. It is a very simple process to file the copyright. www.copyright.gov

Exercise: *Buy or download several scripts of your favorite films. Take a portion of each script (minimum of 10 pages) and study the films to see how closely the scripts match the finished films. Hopefully the scripts you have will be close to the actual shooting scripts they used when making the films. Turn off the sound as you study each film. That's right, turn off the sound. This is one of the greatest tricks in the industry for learning how to shoot and edit. Turn off the sound and simply study the visuals. You will notice so much more visually than you ever have before. The sound is only a distraction to you. Get used to viewing shots without sound, because when you shoot your shots you will not have a soundtrack, sound effects, etc., to sweeten your images and this will help you realize part of the puzzle is missing. Viewing your first shots can be a startling introduction into filmmaking when it doesn't sound as good as what you have been accustomed to hearing. During your edit you will add in the layers of sound effects, music, etc., to sweeten your visual picture.*

CHAPTER 4

Phases of Production

Filmmaking is divided up into three main phases of filmmaking: Pre-Production, Production, and Post-Production. A Development phase exists prior to pre-production and this is where the script is fleshed out/developed prior to starting pre-production. Sales and Distribution follows post-production.

Pre-Production

This phase covers everything that happens prior to shooting the film in order to set everything up for shooting. It involves the most work, because this is where you will make your decisions regarding financing, casting, shooting and marketing your film. This is the planning phase and is the most important phase of filmmaking. Most problems are the result of poor planning. It's like trying to build a house without a blueprint. Plan your film and you will increase your chances of success. If you don't plan it out you will not be successful. A lack of pre-production will almost guarantee failure for your film.

Production

This phase covers the actual on-set filming. Production is the time to bring everything together in an orchestrated fashion. This is why pre-production is so important. Everyone involved in the production phase should be involved in the pre-production phase at some point in order to line everything up. Even the key people involved in the post-production should be involved during pre-production. Do not show up on your film set unprepared. Chaos reins during production so you don't need extra decisions weighing you down by showing up unprepared to shoot.

Post-Production

This phase covers all of the aspects of editing the film in order to produce the finished product.

All three filmmaking phases are related without a clear-cut separation between them, because what you do in pre-production impacts both production and post-production. Editing takes place in post-production, but it is woven throughout your pre-production. Most filmmakers think editing is something to think about after they have finished shooting. Editing is actually the first thing you should be thinking about before you shoot a single shot. You have to know how your film will be edited before you start and you have to know the look of the finished product. What will your film look like on the screen? Film is a visual medium. Visualize your film before you shoot it. A script is only words on a page and it must be translated into visual pictures. Close your eyes and watch your film in your mind. Translate your script into visual pictures. How will all of the pieces fit together to tell your story? Editing relies on how you plan and shoot every shot.

Sales and Distribution

New avenues for film sales and distribution open up every day so it is an exciting time for filmmakers. The days of having to have someone else buy and distribute your film are long gone. A theatrical release into theaters is so competitive that theatrical release may not be a viable option, but you can put your film out there into the marketplace in many other ways. Don't wait until you are done shooting your film to start the business aspects of filmmaking. Development is the time to start generating interest in your film. Possible pre-sales to certain markets are usually done up front. Get the word out that you are making the film. Marketing starts when you start developing the script. Reach out to your audience and connect with them. Send out press releases to the trade magazines and websites and through your social media connections. Develop a buzz!

Pre-Production Topics covered include:
- Budgets, Contracts, Schedules
- Casting
- Production Design
- Equipment
- Insurance, Permits
- Locations
- Shooting Plan
    - Script Breakdown
    - Script Visualization
    - Shot Lists
    - Shooting Schedule
    - Storyboarding
    - Overheads/Layouts
- Blocking/Rehearsing
- Pacing

Production Topics covered include:
- Directing
- Cinematography
- Lighting
- Sound

Post-Production topics covered include:
- Editing

Sales and Distribution topics covered include:
- Press/Promotions
- Distributors
- Film Festivals/Markets
- Self-Distribution and Screening

CHAPTER **5**

Budgets, Contracts & Schedules

Budgets

Your budget is your main concern. Is your script written so it falls within your shooting budget? Most people underestimate the cost of their film and often times run out of money down the home stretch. The most important term involving money is a term called cost avoidance. It means planning so you don't spend a fortune. Rather than trying to raise a ton of money, don't spend a ton of money. Don't spend every dime you have on one film. Live to shoot another day. Your first film may not be a huge success. Your second film may not be a huge success. It may take you many films to be successful, so allow yourself the freedom to shoot many films. If you keep making films then your chances of success increase with each film you make.

If you plan on raising money from outside sources then you will have to work within the business laws just as any company does when raising funds. It can be a very complicated process, but if you have the means then go for it. The sources of financing are endless (investors, crowd funding, credit cards, grants, loans, friends and family, etc.), but what are the odds of a return on the investment? Investors must be made aware of the risks of filmmaking and the realistic possibilities of ever seeing a return on their investment. You will most likely want to form a Limited Liability Company (LLC) to protect yourself, because it limits your liability in case of lawsuits brought against you. In this day and age of lawsuits anything is possible so it is best to play it safe. Someone may claim your film caused global warming.

Develop a business plan to show potential investors. Your plan must include:
- Script
- Cast List
- Crew List
- Credits, bios and resumes of your key cast and crew members
- Proposed Production Budget
- Box Office successes for comparable films
- Distribution potential and avenues
- Marketing Plan and Budget
- Return On Investment (ROI) worksheet

This business package should be well thought out and packaged so it looks professional. Consult with an entertainment attorney specializing in finance if your plan is to use investors to finance your film.

You don't need $50 million or $500,000 to shoot your film. You don't need $100,000 to shoot your film. The majority of filmmakers are stopped dead in their tracks because they wait for financing to arrive or fall out of the sky into their laps. Even Steven Spielberg and Clint Eastwood have had trouble raising money for some of their films. If they have trouble what do you think are your odds of financing your film from outside investors? Get past the financial roadblock and realize you can shoot a film for peanuts. You don't need a cast of thousands and a crew of 30 or 20 or even 10. I've shot two films with crews as small as 2 people. You can do it. Change your mindset away from thinking you need all of these people to shoot your film. Stop waiting for something that may never arrive. Plus, if you don't have a big-name A-List cast, then your chances of raising financing are even less.

Work within your budget by maximizing your time and minimizing your expenses/costs. Beg, borrow and steal (not literally) to get your cast, crew, locations, catering and equipment. Try and get what you can for free. Everyone wants their name in lights so barter. You can often get product placement in your film! Contact anyone who has a product you want to use. You may get products for free and maybe even money. All you can do is ask!

Possible Film Costs

If you are shooting on a shoestring budget then some of these costs will not be part of your budget.

- Script
- Office supplies, copying, postage, etc.
- Legal fees
- Advertising for casting calls, crew calls
- Office rental
- Location fees
- Insurance and permit fees, fire, police, security
- Travel expenses, gas, lodging
- Set construction and associated production design costs, props, furniture
- Renting/buying equipment including camera, sound, lighting
- Cast and Crew salaries
- Makeup, hairstyling
- Costumes
- Food is very important. People will work for free, but not without food.
- Recording media
- Editing, music, prints
- Publicity, advertising expenses for your finished film

Determine your film budget by determining what you need each day: from casting, to rehearsal, to shooting, to editing and all the way to exhibition and distribution. Determine your costs based on your needs. Be conservative and include some margin for error. It's better to overestimate your needs rather than underestimating them.

A word of caution. Many filmmakers have broken the bank by charging to credit cards and spending Grandpa's retirement fund, but this is not recommended. You need to be able to budget your shoot without breaking the bank. There are a few stories of filmmakers being successful financing their films this way, but you never hear about all of the failures. Live and spend to shoot another day. Be realistic and let Grandpa enjoy his retirement.

Contracts

If you are planning on raising money from investors, including your relatives, then you must draw up contracts to define all the possible outcomes of your film. Are you paying your cast and crew? Anyone working on your film must know what they stand to make if your film is a financial success. If you are not going to pay them anything up front then they need to know that. **Put everything in writing**. If your film is a huge success, a complete loss, or anything in between, you need to cover all those different scenarios. Cover your bases. Cover your rear end! People lose their minds when money is involved, especially if a film becomes a success. You don't want a bunch of lawsuits coming your way. Define everything in simple terms in writing. If you make a certain amount of money then how much will each person receive? These contract decisions must include all parties involved in the film. You will most likely offer them deferred payment, which means you don't pay them anything up front. Payment is deferred until you earn back your costs and have extra money to pay them. If you make money they make money. It's very simple. You can give them a flat fee, percentage points or both. Giving percentage points means you give them a percentage of profits after costs. Each point is equal to one percentage point.

Release Agreements - For every person and location you use in your film you need to have a signed release agreement. Have them sign a release allowing you to use them, their likeness, their name, their location, etc., in your film and in your marketing (press and advertising).

Draft examples of a Release Agreement, Location Agreement and Product Placement Agreement are shown, but they are drafts and not considered legal documents. Use a lawyer to draw up legal documents for use in your shoot or buy them on the internet. Curtis Kessinger is not liable for any damages if these examples are used as legal documents.

Release Agreement Example

RELEASE AGREEMENT (Draft)
(Crew/Cast)

Shoot Title: _____

I hereby agree to render my services for $xxx.00 compensation ($xxx.00) and hereby grant to you, your licensees, successors and assigns, the right to use my services and the results and proceeds thereof, and to photograph, film, or otherwise record my physical likeness and image in any manner you desire, to use my name and to record and reproduce my voice and other sound effects for use by you in any medium in connection with the production of the above work or any derivative work thereof, for purposes of inclusion in the work or derivative work thereof, or advertising, promotion, or any other lawful purpose whatsoever. I expressly understand and agree that the results of my services and any such photograph, film, or other recording of my likeness, voice, sound recordings or sound effects or any reproductions thereof and all rights therein, and all results and proceeds of my services or my appearance in connection therewith, including, without limitation, any physical sets, stages, props or other property used in connection with the production of the work and any words, characterizations, other material or dialogue which I have created or conceived of, shall be your sole and absolute property as a work-for-$___-compensation for any and all purposes whatsoever in perpetuity, and you, your licensees, successors and assigns shall have the unlimited right throughout the universe to copyright and publish, exhibit or use said material or any part thereof in any manner you desire in any media whatsoever, including without limitation, audio, visual, audiovisual, pictorial, print and literary media.

I agree that you shall have no liability or responsibility for any equipment provided by me or any damage caused thereby or damage thereto and that I am solely liable and responsible for any and all such damage.

I agree that you shall have sole discretion in determining the extent and manner of use of my services, name, photograph or likeness or anything else granted herein and that you are not obligated in any way to use my services, name, likeness or anything else granted herein or any portion thereof in any medium. I agree that you have sole discretion as to any editing, interpolation, addition, dub or alteration of the work.

I further agree that if by reason of my appearance, statements, actions or use of any material(s) furnished by me for the above-mentioned work, derivative work thereof, or other uses, there is any claim or litigation involving any charge by third persons for violation or infringement of their rights, I will hold you, your licensees, successors and assigns harmless from liability and will indemnify you for any and all losses or expenses arising from the defense of such claims or litigation. I realize that you are relying upon this Release in using me in the making of your work and derivative products, which is at substantial cost to you. I am an adult over the age of eighteen (18) years of age. If not over the age of eighteen (18) my legal guardian's signature applies to this agreement.

I agree not to hold you or the property owners, property renters, local and/or state government liable or responsible for any injury, mental or physical, occurring during the production of the above work. I hold myself solely responsible for any injuries occurring during the production of the above work.

I now waive to you and your successors, assigns and licensees, all personal rights and objections to use of my services and the results and proceeds thereof and of me, my name or my personality in connection with the use of still or motion picture photography and sound recording containing my likeness, photograph and/or voice for any and all motion picture, DVD, video on demand, television (including cable and subscription), magazine, publications, merchandise, and performance thereof, accompanied by any narration and dialogue whatever, and the publicity in connection therewith, and/or for any other trade and advertising purposes for the above-mentioned work.

I have read, understand and agree to the above terms and conditions.

<u>Authorization Signature(s) for:</u>

Talent: _____ Date: _____ Legal Guardian: _____
Printed name: _____ SS#: _____
Printed Name: _____
Witness: _____ Date: _____
Printed Name: _____

Location Agreement Example

<u>LOCATION AGREEMENT</u> (Draft)

Shoot Title: _____

The undersigned, hereby grants to _____ (the "Company") and his employees permission to use the property located at below address (the "Property") for the purpose of photographing and recording certain scenes for a motion picture commencing on or about September 2020 and continuing until completion of all scenes and work required. The permission herein granted shall include permission to use the Property on a mutually agreed upon time for the purpose of making added scenes and/or retakes. The Company agrees to use reasonable care to prevent damage to the Property and the Company will not hold the property owner liable for injury to personnel(crew, talent, etc.)

All rights of every kind in and to all photographs and sound recordings made hereunder (including, but not limited to, the right to exhibit any and all scenes photographed or recorded at and of the Property throughout the world) shall be and remain vested in the Company, its successors, assigns and licenses, and neither the owner nor any tenant or other party now or hereafter having an interest in the Property shall have any right of action against the Company or any other party arising out of any use of said photographs and/or sound recordings whether or not such use is, or may be claimed to be, defamatory, untrue or censurable in nature and they hereby waive any and all rights of privacy, publicity or other rights or a similar nature in connection with the exploitation of any such photographs or soundtracks.

In full consideration of the above, the Company will not pay/will pay the undersigned for use of said Property.

Should the Company elect not to use the Property for filming purposes, written notice will be given prior to the scheduled filming date.

Authorization Signature(s) for:

The Property: _____ Date: _____
Printed name: _____
The Property: _____ Date: _____
Printed Name: _____
The Company: Date: _____
Printed Name: _____
Property Address: _____
_____

Product Placement

If you plan on using any products in your film that you do not have the rights to use you need to get a release form signed by the company owning the product. You can use just about any product if you are not using it in a defamatory way. Product placement has to be covered by a contract for you to use any companies' products in your film. Get their approval before you start production. Do not place any product, location, building, person, copyrighted or trademarked items such as artwork, logos, music, lyrics or dialog without written permission to use it. Get it in writing.

Product Placement Agreement Example

PRODUCT PLACEMENT AGREEMENT (Draft)

Shoot Title: _____

The undersigned, _____, hereby grants to _____ (the "Company") and his employees permission to use a WIDGET ("Product") for the purpose of photographing and recording Scene 19 for a motion picture commencing on or about September 2020 and continuing until completion of all scenes and work required. The permission herein granted shall include permission to use the Product on a mutually agreed upon time for the purpose of making added scenes and/or retakes.

All rights of every kind in and to all photographs and sound recordings made hereunder (including, but not limited to, the right to exhibit any and all scenes photographed or recorded using the Product, throughout the world) shall be and remain vested in the Company, its successors, assigns and licenses, and neither the Manufacturer, Licensee or other party now or hereafter having an interest in the Products shall have any right of action against the Company or any other party arising out of any use of said photographs and/or sound recordings whether or not such use is, or may be claimed to be, defamatory, untrue or censurable in nature and they hereby waive any and all rights of privacy, publicity or other rights or a similar nature in connection with the exploitation of any such photographs or soundtracks.

In full consideration of the above, the Company will not pay/will pay the undersigned for use of said Products.

Authorization Signature(s) for:

WIDGET Product: Date: _____
Printed name: _____
WIDGET Product: _____ Date: _____
Printed Name: _____
The Company: _____ Date: _____
Printed Name: _____

Schedules (call sheets)

Your schedules need to show who, what, when and where for each day of shooting (cast, crew, locations, equipment, props, food). Make up your schedules any way you like so that you understand how and what you will shoot every day of your film production. It's always best to take a conservative approach when scheduling, because shooting always takes longer than you think it will. Practice will help you determine how much shooting you can actually accomplish in one day. Everyone needs to be given these schedules to know what scenes are to be covered and when and where they will be shot. Schedule your cast and crew so you best utilize their time and energy. People don't want to hang around for 10 hours before they are actively involved in the production on any given day. It drains the life and energy right out of them. Plan, plan, plan.

CHAPTER 6

Casting

Finding the right cast and crew will make or break your film. Much depends on the size of the budget you have at your disposal. Can you afford to pay the cast and crew? If the answer is no, then that helps determine who you approach and how you approach them. Union cast and crew will often work for free. Yes, it's true even though they risk fines, suspension and expulsion from their respective unions. It is their responsibility if they want to work for free. Many people will work for deferred payment if they have the possibility of receiving money once the film generates revenue.

You want to cast the best talent you can find. Name cast have a following so that can mean instant ticket sales and a better chance for distribution. Does it guarantee anything? No!

Search everywhere you can for cast and crew talent such as local theaters, college campuses, the internet, union offices, etc. If you live close to a major city you can find a large talent pool. Casting fresh faces are always a pleasant surprise. Talent is everywhere. New people are discovered daily. Ask for headshots, resumes and reels of their past work if they have them. Hold open casting calls if you must. Rehearse with the people who come in to try out. Have them read for you. Let the actors give you their first impression of the roles then direct them if they are off track. If you cannot find the cast you need then cast people who are the part. If you need someone to play a fireman then go cast a real fireman. If your script calls for casting minors understand that working with minors falls under the child labor laws. Know the law!

Whatever it takes...find your cast and crew!

Casting Choices Hierarchy

- Attach star talent. They are always looking for great scripts. Call their agent if they have one. The worst thing they can do is to say no. Go for it! Ask!
- Attach lesser-name talent
- Attach no-name talent
- Attach people who are the part

Once you have determined your cast and crew, it is best to do a table reading where everyone simply reads the script aloud. Record it so you can play it back. Then you will need to **rehearse** and **block** your scenes prior to stepping on the set. Rehearsal is a very important time. Every actor works differently so some like to rehearse and some don't. Find a happy medium that satisfies you. Set up a schedule to rehearse and get everyone together to work on their performances. Don't start shooting until you are satisfied with rehearsals. Also record your rehearsals.

Blocking out your scenes means determining the area of movement for the actors for each shot. Blocking also includes movement of the camera and sound crews. They need to rehearse their moves right along with your cast.

CHAPTER 7

Production Design

Your production design is essentially everything that shows up on screen. Your design must be believable because it creates the realistic world of your film. It starts with the development of visual concepts and proceeds to transforming those concepts onto the sets and locations where you shoot. Production design includes set design, set construction, floor plans (overhead layouts), props, costumes (wardrobe), anything and everything in your shot. Make sure you fill the film frame in your shots if you don't want blank walls or blank sets. Personalize each character's place to match that character. The look of your film sets must match the vision of your film.

Everything on the set should add to and relate to the scenes. Are scenes taking place in the past, present or future? When and where? The audience has to understand this world and it's rules that you are showing them in your film. Always ask yourself, "What is my set doing for this shot/scene?" Don't let the background attract the attention of your audience or hide your subject unless that is your intention. Avoid white walls if at all possible. Darker colored walls provide a better backdrop for shooting as opposed to light colored walls. You'll learn in the lighting chapter that the brightest parts of the frame draw the attention of the audience. If your walls are bright or white then they will draw too much attention away from your characters. Use light, color, movement, etc., to separate the subject from the background. Avoid items poking into the frame that may appear to be sticking out of your subject's head, like telephone poles, trees, etc. unless you want those in your shots.

How you design your sets and what you include or don't include tells the audience a lot about the setting, subject, etc. A wealthy person should live in a mansion with luxury cars in the driveway...everything you think about when the word wealthy comes to mind. A woman in a suit, a man in raggedy clothes pushing a shopping cart down the street, people in uniform...all provide the audience with important information without one word of dialog being spoken. Show it don't say it! The audience sees a doctor and they think about their personal experiences with doctors. Every person in your audience has common ideas about people and those common ideas are what you want to show. Always remember that you can't satisfy everyone, but you sure want to satisfy most of them.

It can be much cheaper and faster to shoot in real places than to build a set to represent a real location. Of course, the problems that can arise while shooting in real locations are numerous, so plan for interruptions. Shooting in a studio or controlled environment limits those interruptions.

Color

Your color choices can have a positive or negative impact on the audience depending on how, when and where they are used. Colors are used to reflect mood, personality, and time of year or time in years. What is the situation? A wild, outgoing character dresses and looks different than a conservative, introverted character. Love versus hate. War versus peace. Happy versus sad. They are all represented by different colors. Colors in contrast create drama (conflict). For example, films shot to look like the early 1900's have a different look than films set in the future. Below is a list of colors and their impact on the audience.

Color	Positive Impact	Negative Impact
Red	Strong, brave, passion	Hot, domineering, aggressive, dangerous
Blue	Strong, trusting, authoritative	Gloomy, depressing, cold
Yellow	Happy, springtime, friendly	Cowardly, soft, weak
Green	Relaxing, alive, tranquil, natural	Greedy (money), jealous, inexperienced
Brown	Warm, earthy, mature, early 1900's	Sad, poor, filthy, cheap
White	Noble, clean, pure, innocence	Sterile, empty, lifeless, cold

The many variations of these colors have different meanings depending on the intensity, saturation and shade of the colors. For example, a pink red is more relaxing than a fire engine red or an orange red. It all depends on the way you use the color with the rest of the subjects in the frame. Color impacts the audience based on how they relate color to their lives. When dealing with colors in your sets, wardrobe and lighting make sure you run test shots to see how it impacts you and others. Don't be afraid to ask others for their opinion.

Steven Spielberg's use of the muted red for the little girl's jacket in *Schindler's List* is a startling use of color. The color represented the braveness and strong hope while the girl continued to hide and avert capture at the hands of the Nazis, but then we learned of her death and that same red turned to a dangerous and evil red, blood red representing the whole Nazi regime and Holocaust. One color had different meanings depending on the situation in which it was used.

The Wizard of Oz used color brilliantly. Dorothy came from a drab brown landscape to this beautiful place. It was a breathtaking view of a better place than she originated from or so she thought. The beauty was misleading in that it posed great danger to Dorothy when she was lured down the yellow brick road. Dorothy soon realized that the brown drab colors of Kansas were much more beautiful and important to her than the colors in Oz. Use color to your advantage, but understand the types of messages your colors may be sending to your audience.

Wardrobe

Make sure you buy two of every wardrobe item in case one item is destroyed or lost. Always keep tabs on your wardrobe. Do not allow the cast to take the wardrobe with them unless they own it and will ensure it will be safe in their hands.

CHAPTER **8**

Equipment

Technology is simply a tool. No matter what format you are shooting on technology will not help you if you don't know what you are doing. Your budget will be your limiting factor in regards to the kind of equipment you can afford to use. This book is not about the latest camera, lighting or editing equipment. Equipment changes daily. You can obtain that information from many different sources. Before you buy, rent or borrow your equipment find out every pro and con from people using the exact equipment you want to use. This book would never have an ending if it tried to cover every possible combination of equipment. The bottom line is this. You can make your film on a $500 camera or a $500,000 camera and the filmmaking aspects are the same. Films shot on $500 cameras have been released in theaters and other venues across the world. Many films shot on $500,000 cameras will never be released in a theater or in any other method of distribution.

Cameras can be bought new or used at great prices. You don't need massive amounts of lighting equipment. You can use household lights, construction lights, etc. Be creative. Don't spend tons of money on equipment. Sound equipment is relatively cheap for a shotgun microphone (mic) and accessories such as windscreens and support equipment. You can even make a mic boom pole out of a paint pole. You can do a lot with very little.

Get the best equipment you can afford. It would be best to use a camera that allows manual control and adjustment of most functions. If it is strictly automatic then you won't be able to get the production values you need. You want to be able to control your camera and not have it control you and the way you shoot. You are often better off buying equipment rather than renting, because it allows you more time to practice and shoot your films. You do not want to rush yourself when filming. Owning equipment allows you tax write-offs if you declare your filmmaking costs as a business. If anyone tells you that you have to buy something, always get a second and third opinion. Always remember it is not about the equipment, it is about the language of film and you the filmmaker.

Formats

Shooting formats change all the time and the next best format is just around the corner.

CHAPTER 9

Insurance & Permits

Insurance and permits are normally required when shooting and they are very expensive for low-budget filmmakers. If you want to buy insurance and permits check with the local film office in the city where you plan on shooting. Once you take out a permit city officials might require you to have a police presence on your shoot in case you need to control crowds or traffic. If you can afford them buy them. If you cannot afford them, it's up to you to determine if you want to shoot anyway! Just Shoot It!

CHAPTER **10**

Locations

Locations can make or break the look of your film. Locations have a visual impact on the audience especially if you can find unique locations to use. Give the audience something they haven't seen before. Keep your locations to a minimum, because moving from one location to another during the course of a day requires costly prep and setup time. Make sure there is adequate parking and facilities to handle everyone and everything.

How much budget do you have? You may need to shoot your film around the locations you can get for free. Do you have a location manager or are you handling the task yourself? Either way scout out your area for locations. Some people will be excited to have you shoot at their location, especially if you use the owners as extras and give them a screen credit. Others will not want you anywhere near their location. Understand that the owners don't want you to disrupt their business or their home. If you shoot at a business location try and shoot during closed hours so you don't disrupt their business income. If you have to shoot during business hours then be prepared for interruptions and plan on compensating them for their time and possible lost business. Once you are done shooting make sure you leave the location as clean as or cleaner than when you arrived.

Know your locations. Figure out what you want out of each location for your scenes. When you plan your shots go to your locations and see if each location meets your requirements for the shots and scenes in your script. What are the limitations of the locations? Are there potential problems with sound in the area? Listen for noises such as traffic, aircraft and any other disruptions that may cause sound recording problems. Listen for interior noises such as refrigerators, phones, air conditioners, elevators, doors, and even lights. If you are shooting exterior shots analyze your locations for lighting. How does the sun move across the location at various times of the day? Do any locations prevent you from getting equipment into and out of the area? Take other people with you. Take your cinematographer, production designer and sound mixer with you. The more eyes and ears the better. Any location limitations will dictate how you arrange your sets and what kind of shots you can and cannot shoot at each location. Take your camera with you and use it as your set of eyes. Looking through the camera is different than simply looking.

Determine the electrical setup for each location. Do you have enough power to handle your lighting? Will you need to bring in an electrical generator? If so where will you park it? Will you disrupt the neighborhood during shooting? If so how can you alleviate any inconvenience to people who live around the location? You must realize they do not have the passion for your film the way you do. Most of them don't care about your grand plans for super stardom. Ask them what you can do to make a possibly bad situation better for them. Hopefully they will respect you for asking and caring.

So many things are happening during Production that you want to make as many upfront decisions as possible. During Pre-Production you will need to develop a shooting plan. The shooting plan is the overall plan for how you will shoot your film. The plan includes a shot list, shooting schedule, storyboards, overhead layouts and production schedules. Some filmmakers use storyboards and overhead layouts and some don't. You will have to make your own decision on whether to use them. They work well for initial visualization of your film.

CHAPTER 11

Shooting Plan

Now that your script is ready it is time to develop a shot list, shooting schedule, production schedule, storyboards, and overhead layouts. Storyboards and overheads are optional for some. The simple definition of a film is it's a bunch of shots! A bunch of shots put together to tell a story.

Shot List

Your shot list is simply a list of the shots you will shoot for each scene in your script. You have to give detailed attention to each shot. You have to figure out how many shots you need and what you want in each shot. What emotion or function does each shot provide to the film? The key is that you have to find the right style of shooting for each scene. You would shoot comedy scenes differently than dramatic scenes and visa versa. Film the person, place, thing, etc., which is most important for that shot at that moment in the script. Write down each shot on a list. There will be disagreements on how best to shoot your shots so be flexible when new ideas arise, which they will as you work through your shots. Everyone has their own opinion. Don't be afraid to make changes. Be flexible.

It's overwhelming trying to think of all the shots you're going to need to shoot, but remember to think of one shot at a time just as you would build your house one nail and one board at a time. Find ways to use shots to relate info rather than spelling it out in obvious ways. If you shoot a shot one way then how do you need to shoot the rest of the shots so they fit (edit) together? Think about your film as a whole and then break it down into shots. Shoot every shot with a plan in mind for the finished product. You can't shoot separate shots and hope they all fit together. A film is a jigsaw puzzle with each piece being created individually, yet each piece has to fit into the puzzle.

Make sure your script has scene numbers in the margins. This is called the shooting script. If your software doesn't allow you to put scene numbers in the margins then you can literally write numbers in the margins. Each time you change locations in your script you would need another scene number. If you were shooting in your home then each room would be another location. You can break up your script any way you wish, but make sure you have a way of keeping track of your shot list with the scenes in your script.

In order to create your shot list the first thing you do is break down your shooting script into the number of shots you will need for each scene. Just as each scene has to count, so does each shot, otherwise there is no reason to shoot it. It must add something otherwise you have to eliminate it. Everyone approaches their script differently. Some people look at the script in three acts. Some break it up into sequences. Some look at it strictly as a bunch of scenes. How you look at your script determines how you break it down. So the breakdown goes from:

- The top level, which is your script
- To the acts making up your script
- To the sequences making up your acts
- To the scenes making up your sequences
- To the shots/elements making up each scene
- To the camera/lighting/sound/equipment setup for each shot/element

By the time you show up on the set you should know what you want in each shot and have everything you need on the set and ready to shoot. Don't attempt to figure it out once you arrive on the set. By that time it will be too late! Plan ahead and come prepared.

SHOOTING PLAN

How do you determine the number of shots? Each scene in your script needs to be analyzed and broken down into its elements, which are the key aspects of the scene such as subjects, setting, info, action, dialog, etc. Each shot focuses on a certain element of the scene. Throughout this book the word **subject** refers to characters, objects or anything in a shot. The number of shots required equals the elements plus coverage. Coverage means shooting extra shots such as reaction shots of characters or other subjects pertaining to the scene, i.e. a gun, ticking clock, storm clouds brewing outside, etc. This coverage allows you more choices during your edit. Coverage allows you to change the pacing of your film by cutting (shorten) or expanding (lengthen) scenes. Often times the words in the script do not translate well onto film. Coverage can help solve some editing problems. Don't be afraid to try different shots, but be selective. A filmmaker has to be able to make decisions about what to shoot and what not to shoot. You cannot shoot every scene from every angle imaginable. You'll never finish shooting. Once you go through the additional chapters in this book you will be able to add the camera choices for each shot into your shot list and understand how to determine the shots you will need.

Each time you shoot the same shot setup (camera position) it is another version or **take**. As soon as you change the setup then it is another shot not another take.

The shot list gives you a forecast of your film and helps you determine how long it will take you to shoot and how much it will cost.

Following is an example of how scenes can be broken down into the required number of shots. Every filmmaker has unique ideas and would shoot different shots for this example. This is simply one viewpoint.

Example: A policeman enters a small church during the service to arrest a criminal hiding out in the congregation. Scene 5 is the exterior of the church prior to the policeman entering. Scene 6 is the interior of the church. Scene 7 is the exterior of the church as more police arrive and a gun battle ensues. Scene numbers change each time you change locations. The location changes when you go from exterior to interior and back to exterior. What are the possible elements you need to shoot?

Policeman, criminal, church, priest, choir, congregation, bible, religious symbols, etc.

Example Shot list:

Scene 5 – Exterior Church
5A - Long Shot of the church as a lone police car skids to a halt
5B - Medium Shot of the same police car skidding to a halt
5C - Close Up as policeman looks around
5D - Medium Shot as policeman rushes from the car, gun drawn, and storms the church

Scene 6 – Interior Church
6A - Long Shot as the policeman bursts into the church, gun drawn
6B - Close Up Shot of shocked reaction from the Priest
6C - Long Shot of shocked reaction from the congregation
6D - Medium Shot as criminal pulls out his gun and starts shooting
6E - Medium Shot as Policeman dives for cover
6F - Long Shot as Congregation panics, people running every direction
6G - Close Up Shot of a bullet piercing a bible
6H - Medium Shot of organist diving behind the organ

Scene 7 – Exterior Church
7A - Extreme Long Shot of church as police cars surround it
7B - Long Shot of the criminal as he runs out with the congregation
7C - Long Shot of Police officers as they fire away
7D - Montage of gun battle
7E - Close Up Shot of the wounded criminal
7F - Long Shot of the criminal, in handcuffs, being carried to an ambulance

As you notice in the above list you place the scene number and then a letter to represent each different shot. It is best to skip the letters "I" and "O" so they are not confused with the numbers 1 and 0. Each take would be **slated** to show the scene number, shot letter and take number. More information on slates is covered later.

Shots 5A, 5B, 5C and 5D could be covered in one shot using a crane shot or other camera movement. If you decided to cover 5A through 5D with one shot, it better work to perfection, because you have no other shots to use during your edit. Now you know why you should shoot additional shots (coverage) to cover yourself in case any part of the combined shot doesn't work. You can shoot shots 5A through 5D as one shot and as separate shots to cover yourself for editing.

Shooting Schedule

Once you have developed a shot list then you have to determine a shooting schedule. The shooting schedule is the shot list rearranged in the order in which you will shoot each shot, since you normally shoot out of sequence. Having a shooting schedule prior to stepping on the set is of utmost importance. This will allow you to plan each day's shoot and ensure the proper equipment, resources, cast, crew, etc., are on the set when you need them there.

Once again let's use the above example of the church scenes to better understand what is meant by a shooting schedule. Imagine that you can't get into the church to shoot the interior shots on the same day you are shooting the exterior shots. You may shoot shots 5A, 5B, 5C, 5D, 7A, 7B, 7C, 7D, 7E and 7F on one day since they are all exterior church shots and then come back another day to shoot the interior shots. And whether you shoot these shots in order depends on other factors. Maybe the actor playing your criminal is only available in the morning on that day so you want to shoot shot 7B, 7D (some of the gun battle), 7E and 7F first thing in the morning. Then maybe shoot 5A, 5B, 5C, 5D, 7A, 7C, 7D (the rest of the gun battle), etc. Do you understand how to determine the shooting order? Many factors come into play. It is not the same as the shot list. Now you also have to think about changing weather and lighting color as the sun rises and sets. Maybe it will be sunny when you shoot shot 5A and then storm clouds fill the sky and you can't shoot any more shots until you have clear skies. If the weather prevents you from shooting the rest of the exteriors then you want to have a backup plan ready for each day of shooting. Think about what can happen so you aren't caught off guard and relying on perfect conditions to accomplish your shooting. Your shooting schedule needs to be as efficient as possible. Maybe you have another location close to the church and you can shoot other scenes that day. You have to look at your shot list, determine when is the best time to shoot each shot and then build your shooting schedule. Prepare for problems before they happen so that when they do you will be ready. Problems will show up when you least expect them.

Make a simple spreadsheet for your shot list, shooting schedule, wardrobe, props, cast, crew, etc., in order to keep track of where and when you shoot each shot and what you need for each shot. You might want to keep notes on each shot in case you need to re-shoot at a later date: lens, angles, camera distance, lighting set-up, etc. Take camera stills, footage or draw diagrams of lighting setups, camera setups, sets, etc., for later reference and re-shoots.

Notice the words **Chip Chart** in the following sample of a shooting schedule. It's best to shoot footage (15 seconds) of a Chip Chart each time you change your recording media and each time you white balance the camera. A chip chart, also known as a Grey Scale, is a reference chart of various shades of grey, which can be used for color correction in post-production. The chart also has additional colors besides grey. White balancing your camera does give a color balance, but is it right and true to the colors you want? If you balance to the wrong white color then it changes all other colors. You can get a chip chart from just about any lab or film provider. If you don't live near a lab then find a lab on the internet and call them up and ask for one. Some color correction may be done on certain scenes and this chart is the standard for color reference. If you can't find a chip chart then shoot without one. If you make a great film the experts will find a way to get the finished product they want.

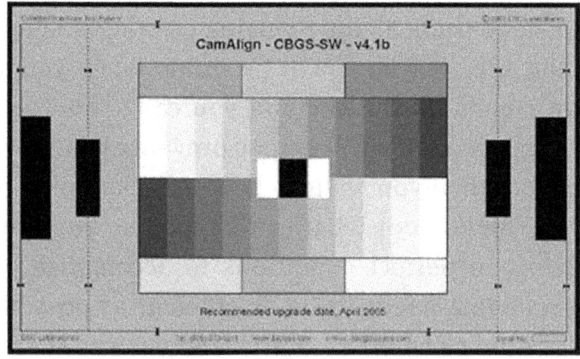

DSC Laboratories

SHOOTING PLAN

Each time you swap out your recording/storage media identify which media number it is so in case you get them mixed up you can identify the correct number. You want to be able to identify each one and also know which shots are on each one. Build all of this into your spreadsheet so that during your edit you know where every single shot and sound is located and can find it in a matter of seconds. It will make your life so much easier.

Sample Shooting Schedule - Notice the shots are not in numerical order like they are on a shot list.

Film: "Midnight Jones"
Date to be Shot: 6/15/2020

Scene	Take	Action
CHIP CHART		
105A	1	LS Charlie exits house
105B	1	MS Charlie approaches car
93A	1	MS Charlie spots Ralph/jumps between hedges to hide
95C	1	CU Charlie crawls to his house
93B	1	CU of Ralph in truck at corner
66A	1	CU Charlie's feet running
91C	1	CU Ralph driving and looking for Charlie

Below is a **sample spreadsheet** showing each shot in shot list order. This gives details of the shots such as camera roll, takes, sound roll, etc. This allows you to know where each shot is located, which shots you liked and didn't like, etc. This is a must for editing. Look at Scene 6. Notice that Shot 6 and Shot 8A were combined into one shot. You may have one shot that covers portions of more than one scene and you can slate it to show all the scenes covered in the one shot. Make sure you understand your scene numbers and the possibilities that exist when shooting.

SCENE #	SHOT	LOCATION	CAMERA ROLL	TAKES	Sound Roll	Take Notes
1	EXT.	Charlie's House	Not shot			
2	EXT	Charlie & Ralph's				
2A		Leonard walks/picks cans at Charlie's house	3	1	MOS	Good take
3	INT.	Bedroom	Not shot			
4	EXT.	Playground				
4A		Master of Little Charlie & Teacher	9	2	3	Both takes good
4B		CU of Teacher	9	1	3	Good take
4C		CU of Little Charlie	9	2	3	Both takes good
5	INT.	Bedroom				
6	EXT.	Ralph's House				
6/8A		Leonard walks to Ralph's trash can	3	1	MOS	Take 1 Ran out of film
6/8A		Leonard walks to Ralph's trash can	4	1	MOS	Take 2 good
7	INT.	Bathroom	Not shot			
8	EXT.	Ralph's House				
8A	see 6	Leonard walks to Ralph's trash can	4	2	MOS	Take 1 Best
8B/F		Ralph confronts Leonard/kids	4	2	MOS	Take 2 Best
8C		Kids screaming	4	2	2	Take 1 Best
8D		Ralph yells at Leonard & Kids	4	2	2	Both takes good
8E		Leonard yells at Ralph	4	2	2	Both takes good

Exercise: *Analyze several scenes from one of your favorite films and break it down into the shots for each scene. How many shots did they use for each scene? What elements of the scenes were covered? Were there additional shots that you thought should have been included or shots that could have been cut from the film?*

Shooting shots out of order requires you to slate each and every shot. Each shot should be identified by using a slate. A slate is a marker board, which serves a dual purpose: one is to identify the scene and shot number, take number, director, etc., so that when you are viewing your footage you know which shot is which. The second purpose is when you record sound on a separate sound recorder, rather than in your camera, you can match up the sound to the camera shots. The slate has a clacker on top of it, which when closed shut provides both a sound syncing mark and a visual syncing (matching) mark in order to sync the image to the sound. If you are recording the sound directly into the camera then you don't need to clack the slate. The slate shown below is a timecode slate.

Denecke, Inc.

A **timecode** slate allows you to automatically apply timecode to your sound media if your sound recorder allows you to manually set the timecode. The same goes for your camera. This timecode can then be used to automatically sync up your sound to your shots by matching the timecode.

Time code was developed by the Society of Motion Picture and Television Engineers (SMPTE). Timecode identifies the exact hours, minutes, seconds and frames of your shots so that when editing you can find an exact frame (or place). If you have two separate shots/sound files with the same timecode then you have a problem. Recording the date along with the timecode allows you to have different timecode for every frame.

Most non-linear editing systems allow you to dial in the timecode and sync up your sound and visuals without having to manually perform this operation using the slate clacker mark. For those filmmakers recording their sound directly into the camera you won't need to sync up the image and sound, nor do you need to use a timecode slate. Your camera should automatically record timecode, but you still need to record different timecode for each frame. You don't want to repeat the same timecode for different shots. Remember that when you change recording media in your camera/sound recorder the timecode will usually start out at zero again. You will need to start the timecode where you left off on the previous recording. So don't forget to reset your timecode.

Slating Tips:

- Hold the slate away from the camera at a distance of 1 foot per 10mm of lens. If you are using a 50 mm lens then you would place the slate 5 ft away from the camera. If you don't know what size lens you are using then basically you want to fill the frame with the slate to make it readable.
- Angle the slate so the light doesn't overexpose it. Angle it down towards the camera, not up into the light.
- Identify the scene #, shot letter, take #, camera media# or sound media #, date, etc. As much info as possible.
- Don't clack the slate for MOS shots (shots without sound).
- Slate a minimum of 5 seconds on camera before starting the action in each scene. 10 seconds is preferred.

Production Schedule

The production schedule shows everything required for each day. Often times people use a physical board with small strips that show what is required each day. It is called a strip board. You can use a spreadsheet or buy one of the many software packages used in the industry. It shows the scene, location, and everyone and everything needed for that scene. You can move the scenes (strips) around in the order you plan on shooting each scene. This allows you to schedule each day. It is like a shooting schedule but it doesn't detail each shot...only what's needed for each shot.

Scene	6	7	5	End Day 1
Day/Night	D	D	D	
Location	C	D	B	
Script Pages	1.5	1	.5	
Bob & Crew				
Police	X		X	
Criminal		X	X	
Congregation		X		
Guns	X	X	X	
Supplies	X	X	X	
Lights	X	X	X	
Windscreens		X	X	

Storyboards

One of the best ways to visualize your film is to develop storyboards. Storyboards are visual representations of shots that help you plan your shoot. You need to develop a good sense of what shots will be required before shooting and plan for some margin of error. Storyboards describe in pictures and words what the script says only in words. Storyboards are a way to communicate ideas to the cast and crew. You may have more than one storyboard for each shot and it is recommended to show key moments in each shot: such as the beginning, middle or end. If drawing/sketching is not one of your strengths then you can use words or stick figures in your storyboards to help you understand what needs to be shot and how it will be shot. You can draw your own storyboards or hire professionals for all your storyboard needs.

Each storyboard should provide a description of the set/location, the camera details and any movement of the camera or subjects. Some filmmakers draw every single shot. Others don't use them at all. You decide if you want to use them or not.

The Art Bunch storyboards

You can add words, direction arrows and any notes to help you in relating your vision for your film. If you want to draw your own storyboards use the blank board sheet provided or make up your own.

SHOOTING PLAN

Blank Storyboard Sheet

Overhead Layouts *(Floor Plan)*

Overhead layouts are simply that...an overhead or blueprint of your sets. These allow you to show movement (blocking) for your shots. They show the set details like furniture placement, subject movement and camera movement. It is similar to a coach drawing up a play.

Shooting Ratio

Shooting ratio refers to the amount of footage you shoot in comparison to the length of your finished film. One page of script usually figures to be one minute on film. If your script is 100 pages long then your film will be 100 minutes long. If your film is supposed to be 2 hours long and you shoot 10 hours of footage then your shooting ratio is 5 to 1. If you shoot 200 hours of footage then your ratio would be 100 to 1. Obviously you want to keep your ratio as low as possible to avoid spending more money than you have to (cost avoidance). Plan your shoot, rehearse and utilize storyboards and overheads to help you keep your shooting ratio to a minimum.

__Exercise__: Read a script of one of your favorite films. Choose several scenes and imagine how the scenes should be shot. Draw some storyboards and overheads for those scenes. Then watch the scenes in the actual film. Were you able to detail the proper information, which would allow you to shoot the shots the way you intended? How did your ideas differ from the actual film?

CHAPTER **12**

Pacing

What is pacing? Pacing is the heartbeat...the pulse...the life of your script and film. Is it slow, medium or fast? Is your pacing correct in the right spots? Your pacing has to change throughout your film so you can keep your audience interested. If the pace is slow then the characters must be exciting. If the pace is fast, action packed, then the characters might have minimal impact. Will the audience be interested in your film or not? The audience has to be glued to the screen. Since you want to take your audience on a roller coaster ride, the pacing has to vary throughout your film, up and down and around. If you stick to one pace, whether it is fast or slow, the audience will lose interest. Pacing is finalized during your edit, but the script had better have great pacing or you won't have anything to work with by the time you get to your edit. Things have to happen! Two people talking for two hours is not something interesting unless the dialog is incredible! It can be done! Skip the boring parts and include the excitement. Excitement doesn't necessarily mean action. Throwing car chases and explosions into the film doesn't mean excitement. Dialog can be exciting if the audience is involved. Get to the emotions of the audience. Get their hearts pounding. Emotional scenes are much more exciting than action scenes lacking emotion. Finding a way to get the audience riding up, down and around on an emotional roller coaster is the key to great film pacing. How long should each shot be? A shot should only be held long enough to make the point you are trying to make.

Exercise: *Analyze footage of your favorite films and time the length of at least 20 to 30 scenes within each film. Compare the quick- cutting style films versus the style of classic films, which allowed the camera to stay on a subject or in a scene longer than most films shot today. Why are scenes exciting to you? Keep track of how many times you laugh or cry or get emotionally involved over the length of a film. Write down your different emotions. How many different emotions did you experience? Could there have been more or less? Should there have been more or less? Should certain emotions have lasted longer during certain parts of the film?*

CHAPTER **13**

Directing

A film is a director's vision of a script. The director must be able to communicate that vision so everyone understands it, because a film is a collaborative effort by everyone involved. A director has to be a Jack-of-all-trades: part actor, part editor, part designer, part cinematographer, etc. Especially on low-budget shoots where you may be the writer-producer-director-cinematographer-editor. Close your eyes and visualize/imagine every scene and every shot until you know exactly what you want. Visualize your film in your head then bring it to life on the screen. If you can see it then you can shoot it. You must know how one shot will connect/transition to the next shot.

The key is being able to tell a great story and get to the root of your film, which is emotion! Use your vision to bring out the emotions of your audience and provide them with a powerful, emotional journey. Use cinematography to enhance the emotions of the characters. Know how you want to compose your shots to convey the message to the audience.

The director's main focus, while on the set during production, is working with the actors. Your **actors** (term includes actresses) bring your script to life. Each character has to act as if they are the most important subject in each scene and you have to bring out their best performance. Great images without great performances will not hold up, but great performances without great images can still be great. Great performances mean doing, not explaining. Give your characters the motivation to take action. Give them the why not the how. They have to know their goal in each scene. They have to know what they want. They have to know their character's back story to know what approach to take. Make it simple for the actors to do their job. Everyone is unique so one approach will not work for every actor. You want your actors to be as free and natural as possible. Let them do their part and let the camera record them doing their part. Sometimes blocking can limit the actor's freedom. Give them some range to act. Let them act. Don't close them in with too many constraints. They aren't mimes in a box.

If you have a great script that makes logical sense, the actors can feel great about acting the part. If they do not fully believe in the part then they will not fully reveal the character. You also have to have them in the right set, right costume, right light, right cast, right everything in order to fully realize the character. They look to you for the vision and direction in which they are heading. Tell them what you like about their performance and then give them adjustments. What the actors need from the director is **why** they are to act a certain way? Don't tell them to be sad. They need to know why they are sad. Don't tell them exactly what to do, tell them what is going on and how it impacts them. Telling them to be sad is not directing. It's demanding. If instead you told them, "Your favorite pet has to be put down and you will not get to say goodbye beforehand." That is motivation. Don't tell them to be angry. Tell them why they should be angry. What is driving the anger? Direct them by motivating them to get the response you want. This is about emotions. "Show me elation," is not directing. "You just won the lottery or met the person of your dreams," is motivation for elation. Each portion of your script should provide the background for the actors. If not, then you will have to provide it. You have to know the point of each shot and scene and know the emotions you want for each shot and scene. If you want performances to be real then you have to let the actors do their job. Provide an environment for them to perform. Don't intimidate anyone. If you are dealing with people who are not actors then you may have to give them more direct performance instructions, but their performance will be more external than internal. Your script must be written for your characters to take action not to talk about or explain about taking action.

Directing is Leadership

The director's attitude is extremely important during production. Try and maintain a positive attitude at all times. When the bullets are flying you must not flinch. You are at the helm of the ship. You are conducting the orchestra. Provide a feeling of security and support for your cast and crew. They want to work in a safe environment that allows them to do their best creative work. People work best when they enjoy their job and the people they are working with. They don't want to be looking over their shoulder fearing the wrath of the director or anyone else on the set. Provide that kind of environment because film is a collaborative undertaking. Everyone is there to support your vision. Everybody has to be working on the same page. They'll do their part if you provide them with what they need. Directors have to be problem solvers on the set. You must be able to make decisions when the pressure is on and everyone is standing around looking at you to make the right decisions. Directors have to be able to work with people. Some don't respect the people they work with. You have to like and respect people. Your people are your most important asset so treat them that way. Support them. You are nothing without your cast and crew. Don't take the attitude that they are nothing without you. You are nothing without them. If you work well with your team then things will go much more smoothly. Make your set a comfortable place for everyone to do their part. If you're uptight they're going to be uptight. If you can put everyone at ease your chances of success increase. You are the one at the top so you have to be the most positive, the most trustworthy and give all the praise and success to everyone else. If your shoot is a failure it is your fault. If your shoot is a success it is because of everyone else. Don't be afraid to take the blame and to give out the credit. You'll go far knowing and implementing those two things on your movie set.

Be confident in your decision-making and be secure enough to allow others to provide their input. Their input is gold! Involve them. Work with them to better your film. Ruling with an iron fist and a closed mind will cause problems. You want the end product to turn out better than the script...better than anyone imagined. Production can be chaos. The weather may cause delays and force you to rush to get shots. Actors may not be performing up to your level of expectations. Your crew may not be giving you the look and feel that you want. You may be making the wrong decisions or not making any decisions at all. Many things can go wrong. **Rule number one**...never yell at anyone. You are the leader. Lead by example. Never yell at anyone. Even if they are yelling at you, you have to keep a cool head. Once your voice is raised in anger it is no longer a discussion, it is an argument. Nobody wins an argument. You are the CEO of the film. Act like it. **Rule number two**...praise in public and discipline in private. Give all the praise to everyone else. If you have to discipline someone then do it in private. No one likes to be put on the spot or embarrassed in front of others. Take them aside if you need to, but always show respect for people. If you made the decision to hire them then accept the blame if they do not perform up to your standards. You made the mistake of hiring them. Either work with them or find their replacement. That is your responsibility.

You have to lead and know the others are doing their part. Leadership centers on relationships and communication. Diffuse tension that arises on the set and communicate with everyone. If you are not speaking the same film language there will be problems. You will have to deal with many things going on all at once. You have to be able to make decisions. If you are tentative, people will take advantage of your lack of decision-making skill and turn your film into their film. Start in pre-production by working with everyone who will be present on the set. If you have a producer make sure everything needed by your cast and crew has been taken care of prior to shooting. If you are the producer, which is very likely, you have to ensure everything is in place when it needs to be.

Cinematography

Cinematography entails taking the vision of the director and putting that vision onto film. In other words, find the best way to shoot your shots. If you are the cinematographer on your film then this job falls into your hands. The cinematographer is also referred to as the Director of Photography or DP. This book is intended to teach you how to perform the tasks in order to shoot your film. Since your script is unique, your film must be unique. You would not shoot every film with the exact same look. Create the visual look that is right for your film at that moment. As things change so does your shooting.

There are many theories and methods for shooting, but the bottom line is getting the meaning of your film across to the audience. Find ways to let the audience think for themselves. For example, instead of shooting a scene showing a man being fired, shoot shots of him trying his key in his office door and it won't work...his parking spot has been painted over...security escorts him off the premises. Those simple shots provide the audience with the story meaning. You don't have to spell everything out. This type of shooting requires much more thought than the average film, but it is well worth the effort. Get creative and set yourself apart from the rest of the competition.

In order to choose the correct images for your film you will be making many camera and shooting decisions: focus, frame rate, lighting, contrast, camera movement, character movement, lenses, composition, type of format (film, digital, animation, 3-D, etc.), texture, tone of the scene, camera distance from subject, point of view, angles, color, rhythm, pacing, etc. You also have to consider how each shot relates to the shot that comes before it and the shot that will come after it in the edited film. By the time you finish this book and spend time practicing with your camera you will fully understand how to make the right decisions. Remember to practice, practice, practice.

Now you have to determine how to tell the story using the camera. The audience doesn't want to notice the camera. They simply want the story. Knowing how to shoot your shots to impact the audience's emotions is a powerful tool. Also remember that each character might be treated differently by the camera and lighting choices, etc.

Each shot requires at least **7 decisions** involving the camera.
1. What lens will you use? This refers to the focal length of the lens.
2. How far will you place the camera from your subject? Most shots are done within a 4-14 foot range.
3. What will be the Vertical Camera Angle in relation to the subject? This means the height of the camera? Will the camera be below the subject, above the subject or even with the subject?
4. What will be the Horizontal Camera Angle? Will the camera be straight on in regards to the subject or at an angle? How much of an angle?
5. Will the camera be moving (dynamic) or not (static)? What kind of movement? One moving shot might be able to cover what would take several static shots.
6. What will be in focus and what will be out of focus? Will you use soft focus, hard focus, etc?
7. How will you expose your shots? Normal, underexposed or overexposed?

You will be composing each shot using your film knowledge. Very little is new when making a film. It has already been done so study similar films and use what they've done. Learn from the best. You are not going to reinvent the wheel...improve on it.

***Exercise:** Analyze one of the Coen Brothers' films. No one shoots a film quite like they do. Their camera decisions are as interesting as in any film. It is not there for show. It serves its purpose in telling the story. Don't forget* *to mute the sound. Take notice of when they move the camera or when it's static. Notice their subject movement. Notice how they visually tell their stories.*

People have coined the phrase "fix it in post" which tends to mean don't worry about shooting the film correctly...just shoot it and then when they do post production they will correct any errors and make the shots look the way they wanted in production. Don't support that philosophy. That is like saying you can fix the house once you have already built it. Get it right the first time or it will never be right. Get the original cinematography right. Don't think you can fix it in post. That is the wrong approach to take. Can you fix some things in post? Sure you can, but do you have the time, money and expertise? Maybe you do, but do you want to spend your money foolishly?

CHAPTER **14**

Camera Lenses

It is time to help you to determine camera choices for each shot. If you have 20/20 vision then your eyes are the perfect lens, because everything is in focus for all distances away from you. You can see things far away and up close. A camera lens is just the opposite. It doesn't see what your eyes see. It can perfectly focus on only one specific point a certain distance away. All other points in all directions get more out of focus the further away they get from that one specific point. Your eyes can see all points in focus, but the camera can't. If you want to shoot something 1 foot away from the lens and then 200 feet away from the lens, you will have to refocus and may have to change to a different lens between shots. Start thinking about what the camera lens sees, not what your eyes see.

There are two physical types of lenses: **zoom** and **prime**. Most everyone is familiar with a zoom lens. Most cameras come with a standard zoom lens. Lens sizes (focal lengths) are measured in millimeters (mm). What is the definition of focal length? You had to ask didn't you? The focal length of a lens is the distance from the film plane to the optical center of the lens. That probably confused you as it does most everyone. It's not important to know nor is it something you need to remember, but since you asked…there it is.

Zoom Lens

A zoom lens is adjustable and covers a range of focal lengths. For example 12mm-120mm or 50mm-300mm. The zoom lens has many different lens elements built into it in order to cover the range specified on the lens. On top of the normal zoom range some digital cameras might have optical zoom capability. Zoom lenses are usually not as sharp as prime lenses, due to light loss in the lens elements, but most people would not notice the difference. Now you know why professional photographers and cinematographers are constantly switching lenses when shooting. They use mostly prime lenses not zoom lenses. Don't let this bit of information influence your choice of lenses in any way. Shoot with whatever you have available.

Prime Lens

A prime lens has one fixed focal length. For example a 10mm, 25mm, or 50mm lens, etc. A prime lens usually produces sharper images than a zoom lens.

A quick note about **lens care**. Never blow on a lens with your own breath. Use a small blower (hand held) or camel hair brush for dust, dirt and small marks. Never use alcohol, swabs, facial tissue or clothing to wipe a lens. Use proper lens care materials: lens cleaner and lens tissue paper. The lens tissue should be rolled up like a cigarette and used without lens cleaner first. Then if the lens needs additional cleaning apply a small amount of cleaner on the tissue and clean the lens. Do not squirt cleaner directly on the lens itself. The cleaner can seep into the lens flange area and degrade the sealant securing the lens to the lens body.

Most lenses have two moving rings on them. A **focus** ring and a **f-stop** ring.

Focus Ring

The focus ring obviously controls the focus of your shot. Film cameras have a manual focus ring. Most digital cameras have a servo-controlled focus ring and an auto focus button, but be very careful when

CAMERA LENSES

using auto focus. If your camera is set on auto focus it may continue to search for something to focus on and your shots may go in and out of focus. Ensure the camera is focusing on the subject that you intend to focus on. Some cameras allow you to set them on manual focus but still allow you to use the auto focus button to focus. Know your camera. Practice, practice, practice. Shoot, shoot, shoot.

There are **three methods of focusing a lens**. These methods are listed in order of preference:
- Tape Measure - The best lenses have a focus ring with focus distances measured in feet or meters. This type of focus ring allows you to measure the distance from your camera to your subject using a tape measure and then set your focus ring to that exact distance. This is the preferred method, but some lenses do not have distance settings on the focus ring. Distance settings allow you to change focus more accurately during a shot. This is the job of someone called a **focus puller**. They pull (change) focus during a particular shot, which means as the subject moves closer or further from the camera, they adjust the focus accordingly. If you have distance markings on the lens then you can place pieces of colored tape on the floor and on the camera so they correspond to the distance measurements. As the characters near the colored tape on the floor the focus puller adjusts the focus to match. Distance markings on your focus ring simplify your shooting.
- Eyesight - Using your eyesight to focus means looking through the camera eyepiece and setting the focus. This takes a much more trained eye. You must set the eyepiece to match your eyesight. Everyone else who will focus the camera in this manner must first adjust the eyepiece to match their eyesight. If it's not adjusted for each person it would be the same as you wearing someone else's glasses. Their glasses were not manufactured to match your eye. Each camera eyepiece should allow you to adjust it for your eye so that when you look through the eyepiece and focus the lens, the shot will be in focus.

- Auto Focus Button - The camera does the focusing for you, but you must ensure it focuses on the correct subject and not something in the foreground or background.

Focus Every Shot

Focus the lens before shooting each shot or your shots will most likely be out of focus. The focus may also have to change within a shot if your subject or camera moves. Remember you initially focused the camera for a certain distance from the subject. If that distance changes during the shot, you have to adjust the focus as you are shooting. Rehearse your shots. Determine what you want to be in focus or out of focus. For most shots you don't want everything in focus, because you are directing your audience to look in a certain area. Audiences automatically look at the area most in focus. If you shift the focus then you shift the audience's attention onto your new focus point. Horror films use this technique to perfection. Your teenage couple is in the woods in perfect focus and then you see something blurry behind them. Suddenly the focus shifts to reveal the killer and it's all over for Biff and Buffy! This is called **selective focusing**. You are selecting the point of focus and thus selecting the area you want your audience to notice. If something in the background is in focus and it shouldn't be it catches their attention and they may miss what you wanted them to concentrate on. You want the audience to see what you are trying to show them. This area is called the **Center of Interest** and will be discussed in a later section. Focus is one of the ways you get the audience to look at your Center of Interest.

Depth of Field

Depth of Field refers to what is in focus even though only one point/distance is in perfect focus. For each shot you pick a focus distance and subjects in front of and behind that focus distance will be partially in focus. The further you get from that one point/distance in either direction the less everything will be in focus. You have perfect focus at one point...one distance from the camera and all other points/distances are less in focus.

A depth of field chart is used to determine the focus range for a certain lens size. Do you absolutely have to use a chart? No.

For example if you want to focus on a subject 10 feet away and you are using a 50mm lens, how much area will be in focus? Assume the depth of field chart for that lens, focused at 10 feet, shows a depth of field of 15 feet. Then 1/3 of the distance (5 feet) will be in focus in front of the subject and 2/3 (10 feet) will be in focus behind the subject. 5 feet in front and 10 feet behind. Focusing on the subject 10 feet away, the depth of field is 5 to 20 feet or a total of 15 feet will be somewhat in focus. Your focus distance is 10 ft, but everything from 5 to 20 feet will be somewhat in focus. The focus will decrease the further away you get from the focus point. Other factors come into play such as the exposure setting (f-stop) and the speed of the lens, but for practical purposes this is what you need to know to understand depth of field. If you don't have access to depth of field charts/tables then all you have to do is look through your camera lens to see what is in focus and what is not. Shoot and study footage to educate yourself on depth of field.

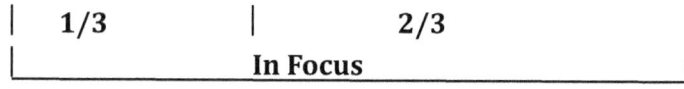

Ken Kiser

If the subject moves towards or away from the camera during the shot then you would need to adjust the focus as the distance between the camera and the subject changes.

If you have two subjects in your frame that are at different distances from the camera, where should you focus? Remember only one distance can be in perfect focus. If you want both subjects to be focused the same, neither of them will be in perfect focus. The perfect focus distance will be somewhere in between them. You will pick a point in between the two so that both will be equally focused. If one subject is 10 feet away and the other is 25 feet away then maybe the focus point will be 16 feet. It depends on the lens you are using. Experiment with your camera so you know your lenses and how they focus.

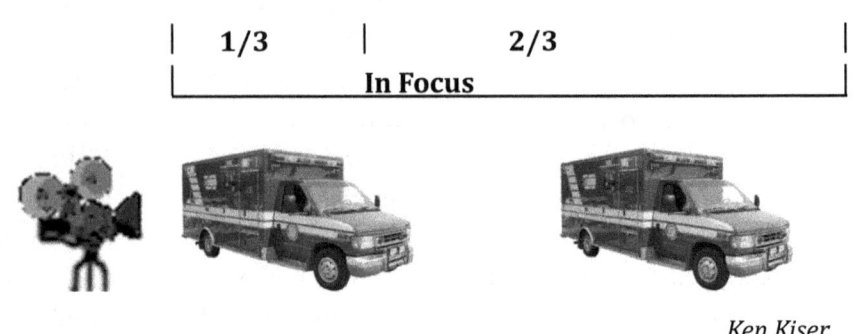

Ken Kiser

Depth of field depends on several factors regarding the lens characteristics and settings.

- F-stop
- Focal Length
- Focus Point

If you want to <u>increase</u> the amount of your shot that is in focus (increase the depth of field of your shot):

- You can switch to a wider angle lens (shorter focal length)... maybe a 25mm instead of 100mm.
- You can move the camera farther away from your subject, meaning your focus distance is greater, and your depth of field is greater.
- You can stop down or close the lens aperture (larger f-stop ring setting), which lets in less light.

If you want to <u>decrease</u> the amount of your shot that is in focus (decrease the depth of field of your shot):

- You can use a longer lens (longer focal length).
- You can move the camera closer to your subject, meaning your focus distance and depth of field are less.
- You can open up the lens aperture (smaller f-stop ring setting), which lets in more light.

With a decreased depth of field, meaning less is in focus, your focus must be more exact than with an increased depth of field. You have less room for error and focus errors will be more obvious. Does that make sense? The less depth of field the more critical your focus becomes. You have less room to play with. The wider the lens the more depth of field and the longer the lens the less depth of field. Focusing using a longer lens is more critical than using a wider lens. Wider lenses give you more leeway in shooting. Some filmmakers use mostly wide lenses for that reason.

Check with the manufacturer of your lenses to see if they have depth of field charts. If they don't then keep shooting and studying to understand how your lenses react to different settings.

One thing to keep in mind when you are shooting two shots that will be edited together is that if you end the first shot by going out of focus, then you would want to begin the second shot out of focus to match. This would provide a smooth transition from the first shot to the second shot.

Exercise: *Analyze 10 to 20 minutes of one of your favorite films. Remember to turn off the sound. Look to see what is in focus and what is not. Is everything in focus in each shot? Do they change the focus (pull focus) during any shots to reveal new information or direct your attention to a certain area of the frame? Do they use selective focusing? Study the parts of the shot that are in or out of focus. View the same shots again and look at parts of the frame from where you would normally look. What do you see that you never saw before? How far do you suppose the camera is away from the subject? Does the focus change during movement of either the subject or the camera or both? Use your camera to shoot various subjects and change the distances, lenses and depth of field. Analyze your footage.*

As mentioned earlier the other moving ring on a lens is the f-stop ring.

F-stop Ring

The f-stop ring may also be referred to as the exposure ring since it determines the exposure of your shot. The f-stop ring controls the lens aperture (opening), which controls the amount of light entering the lens and exposing the recording media. This is the infamous term f-stop, which is a measure of the amount of light. People run and hide when they hear the term f-stop, but it is nothing to fear. It's simply a setting for your lens in order to determine the amount of exposure you want in each shot and whether you want the shot to look normal, underexposed or overexposed. You don't need to know definitions of the f-stop numbers (1, 1.4, 2, 2.8, 4, 5.6, 8, 11, 16, 22, etc.) or how they were developed. All you need to know is that the higher the number...the more light that is present in your shot from your lights (or daylight)...and the smaller the lens aperture setting would be, because you don't need to let a lot of light into the lens.

Let's make this as simple as possible. If you are going to shoot a shot of your subject's face and you have it lit just the way you want it. Then you measure the amount of light on their face, using a light meter, and let's say the measured f-stop is f8. That is the f-stop setting (f8) you would set on your camera lens to show their face the way it is currently lit. Anything in the shot with more light would be overexposed and anything in the shot with less light would be underexposed. If you set the f-stop on your camera lens to f16, which means you close down the lens opening and let less light into the lens, how do you suppose your subject's face would appear? Their face would be underexposed due to less light. If you set the f-stop on your camera lens to f2 then you would be letting more light into the lens and their face would be overexposed. Does this make sense? To simplify this even more...measure the light on your subject, then set your lens f-stop ring to match.

Now if you look at your subject's face and determine it needs more light then you would add more light and your f-stop setting would be greater. This is how you determine the exposure of all the areas of your shot/frame. You have to light all the areas of the frame according to how you want them to turn out based on the camera lens f-stop setting. Maybe you want to underexpose or overexpose your subject's face

CAMERA LENSES 91

compared to other subjects in the shot. You would do this by changing the amount of light, changing the lens f-stop setting or both.

If you have three subjects in the frame and want them to have the same exposure (same f-stop reading) then they must have the same amount of light on them. Each light reading would have to match. If they didn't match then you would have to increase or decrease the amount of light for the three subjects until they have matching light readings. If you wanted one subject to be overexposed then you would add more light to that subject.

Lighting is the most time-consuming portion of production. Know what kind of lighting you want for each shot before you arrive on the set. Lighting choices will be covered later in the Lighting Chapter.

Measure the amount of light you have by using a light meter.

Sekonic Light Meters

Two types of readings can be used depending on where you want to measure the light.

- **Incident reading** is a light reading taken from the position of the subject. The meter is held directly in front of the subject and pointed back at the camera lens. This shows what the camera lens sees when aimed at the subject. This type of reading is the most widely used for f-stop settings. To check the amount of light at any spot in the frame hold the meter at each spot and point it back at the camera.
- **Reflected reading** is a light reading taken from the position of the camera and the meter is pointed back at the subject. This

reading is used to get a general reading of the whole area of the frame. It doesn't allow an individual light reading for each element in the frame like an incident reading does.

The figure below shows the relationship between f-stops, the amount of available light for an exterior shot, and the lens opening sizes. A full sun at noon provides a high f-stop reading of f22 (or greater). To expose the shot normally you would set the lens opening/aperture (f-stop ring) to f22. This means the lens opening is very small, because a large amount of light is available and you don't need to let much light into the lens. If you don't have much light such as a moonlit night and the light reading measures f1.4 you would need to open the lens up in order to let in more light. This is an exaggeration, because a quarter moon would not provide you with enough light to shoot with most lenses.

F-Stop	1	1.4	2	2.8	4	5.6	8	11	16	22
Amount of Light		🌙								☀
Lens Opening Size		◯ (large)								◯ (small)

CAMERA LENSES

- Smaller f-stop means little available light in the scene and a large lens aperture to let in more light.
- Larger f-stop means more available light in the scene and a smaller lens aperture to let in less light.

Stopping down the lens means closing down the lens opening, thus decreasing light entering the lens. The human eye operates in the same manner. Walk out of a dark movie theater into a bright sun and your eye closes down (adjusts) to eliminate some of the light. You are going from a lower f-stop to a higher f-stop setting on your eye.

The amount of light in between f-stop settings is half as much light as the previous f-stop. So f8 lets in half as much light as f5.6 or f5.6 lets in twice as much light as f8.

F-stops do not take into account light lost within the lens itself due to light reflecting off the lens. The term t-stop does take into consideration this lost light. In the ideal situation or for a perfect lens the f-stop would equal the t-stop. Don't worry about t-stops and lost light. The term is only being mentioned in case you hear the term at some point in your long filmmaking career.

Lens speed refers to the widest opening (aperture) or the smallest f-stop setting of the lens.

Speed f4.0 - A slow lens needs more light to properly expose the recording media. F4.0 minimum

Speed f1.0 - A fast lens needs less light to properly expose the recording media. F1.0 Minimum

The f-stop discussion can be very confusing to you at first, but once you start shooting and noticing the f-stop numbers on your light meter or camera it will start to make sense.

Exercise: *Take your camera outside on a sunny day and shoot some footage at different f-stops so you will have normal, over-exposed and under-exposed images. Take notes on the different f-stops you shoot for each shot. Place several objects in different areas of light and shoot at different f-stops to see how your camera reacts to different settings. Shoot at different times of the day, taking notice of the sun positioning in the* *early morning, noon and late afternoon. The sun is very harsh at noon, providing very hard light. Take note of the harsh shadows it casts, especially in a subject's eye sockets and under their nose and chin. Make sure the sun does not shine directly into the lens itself otherwise you will have lens flares. Maybe you want lens flares as an effect in your shot. Most likely you don't. You will need to shade the lens from the direct sunlight or any lights shining directly into the lens if you don't want flares. Shoot indoor footage as well using different lights.*

CHAPTER **15**

Lens Sizes

Now it's time to discuss the lens sizes (focal length) and the impacts on the audience. Lens size determines how much of your subject is in your frame. Lenses fall into three different size categories: wide, normal and long. A wide lens has a wide angle of view as shown in the diagram. A normal lens has a smaller angle of view and a long lens has a very narrow angle of view.

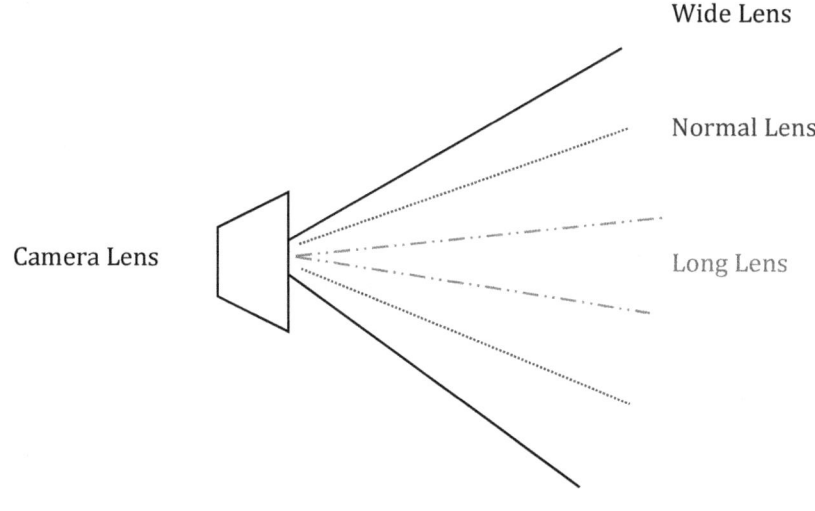

For each shot you have to choose the lens size that best represents/shows the space/angle of view you want. Of course it all depends on how you want to impact the audience.

Check with your specific camera guide/manufacturer prior to shooting to determine what they consider wide, normal and long lenses.

Wide Lens (Short)

A wide focal length lens is also called a short lens. Wide lenses make the subjects appear as if they are smaller and farther away than they actually are because you are shooting a wide area. Short distances look longer and larger, space or areas look larger and more open, and subjects look smaller in relation to the area they are in. Subjects appear isolated and less important in their setting. If a subject is actually 10 feet tall and 10 feet away then it will appear 5 ft tall and 20 ft away. Wide lenses give the greatest depth of field, which means more of your shot is in focus. Movement towards and away from the camera looks faster than it actually is (moving 20 mph looks like 40 mph). Lateral (sideways) movement in front of the camera looks slower than it actually is. A wide lens decreases chaos, tension and action, except when things are moving towards or away from the camera. Wide lenses have a more settling impact on the audience. Wide lenses are also used in comedy films to distort facial features when shooting a close up of a subject.

Normal Lens

A normal focal length lens makes things look normal. They show reality with no distortion of space or movement. The area looks normal size. Movement towards, away from, and laterally in front of the camera appears as it actually is in real life. If a subject is 10 ft tall and 10 ft away then it will appear 10 ft tall and 10 ft away.

Long Lens (Telephoto)

A long focal length lens is also called a telephoto lens. A long lens magnifies subjects (like a telescope or pair of binoculars) by making them appear larger and closer than they actually are in real life. If a subject is 10 ft tall and 10 ft away it will appear 20 ft tall and 5 ft away.

They have a narrow angle of view making everything feel and appear claustrophobic and confined. A long lens increases chaos, tension and action. Long lenses are often used for city street scenes because they compress things together and can make 10 people look like a crowd or 10 cars look like a traffic jam. Things appear flatter than normal due to the compression effect. Movement towards and away from the camera appears slower than it actually is (moving 20 mph looks like 10 mph). Lateral movement in front of the lens appears faster than it actually is. You have less depth of field meaning less is in focus, allowing you to block out the background or foreground. Long lenses allow the camera to be farther away from the subject than wide or normal lenses. For example if you wanted to show a stampede of buffalo approaching a small child you could compress the actual distance they are apart from each other by using a long lens. This allows you to place the child a safe distance from the animals, but make it appear as if they are bearing down on top of the child. Someone throwing a punch, towards the camera, at another person could miss by 12 inches, because a long lens makes it appear as if the punch connected.

Make all lens choices based on what you want to show in your shots. Do you want to drive your car 90 miles per hour around a mountain curve? That would be too dangerous. You could use a wide lens and drive 35mph and make it appear as 90 mph coming toward or away from the camera and then use a long lens for the lateral movement in front of the camera. Do you want your small room to appear larger? Use a wide lens. Are you shooting in an open area and want it to appear smaller? Use a long lens. Do you need to block out certain areas of a shot? Use a long lens. Do you want everything to appear normal? Use a normal lens. Determine what you want and then choose your lens.

__Exercise__: Analyze footage of your favorite films and notice the different shots. Look for the space that each shot represents. Does the shot show an open area, normal looking area or a small narrow area? Is there any comic distortion in any of the shots? Do shots feel claustrophobic? Is movement exaggerated or slowed down? How do the shots make you feel? Can you *determine what kind of lens they used for each shot? In a short amount of time you will be able to determine which lens was used for each shot.*

Where you place your camera also figures into how much area you cover. Many filmmakers set the camera down then figure out what lens to use. This is the wrong approach. You must know why you are placing your camera in a certain spot. Determine the lens you want to use then determine where to place the camera. Not the opposite.

If you need to <u>increase</u> the size of your subject...for example you want to double the size of your subject.

- Use the same lens and move the camera twice as close to your subject. Your subject size will double, anything closer to the camera than your subject will be more than double in size and anything behind the subject (farther away) will increase in size, but will be less than double in size.
- If you keep the camera where it is and double the lens focal length (i.e. use a 100 mm lens instead of a 50mm lens) then <u>everything</u> in the frame will be double in size.

Making one or both of the changes will impact the look of your shots.

To <u>decrease</u> the size of your subject, do the reverse of the above. Move the camera farther away, decrease the lens focal length or both.

What happens if you move the camera closer to the subject, but decrease the focal length? Or move the camera farther away, but increase the focal length? The possibilities are endless, but you will only learn by shooting, shooting, shooting.

*<u>Exercise</u>: Find several objects. Place them at different distances from your camera so you can visually see how the different focal length lenses change the object sizes and their relations to one another. For the first series of shots place the camera in one spot then shoot 30 seconds of footage with a wide, normal and long lens. For the second series of tests use the same lenses and move the camera closer and farther away from the object. For the third series of shots change the focal length of the lens **and** move the camera closer and farther away from the object. Remember to focus every shot.*

Reward Time

You deserve a reward for getting through this much material and doing the exercises. Always reward yourself along the way to your goals. Enjoy the trip, because the trip is 99% of the goal.

Composition

Composition is simply the way you arrange everything in the film frame for each shot. Composition determines the look of your shots and the look of your film. You will learn how to compose each shot and know how your composition impacts the audience.

Composing a static shot is easy compared to composing a shot with both camera and subject movement. You need to understand how composition changes once you add movement into your shooting. Composing with movement is called Dynamic Composition.

Film is 2-dimensional, but you want to compose your shots so the audience sees depth, dimension and contrast. Add depth by placing subjects in the foreground and background and use light to highlight them. Add dimension by shooting subjects from angles. Add contrast using color and light. You want to fill the frame in your shots, but do not overfill the frame and distract your audience. Keep things as simple as possible. Not filling the frame also has a meaning. It can show your Main Character is struggling: signs of despair, loneliness, oppression, etc.

Your main goal is to get your story across to the audience. Compose your shots so they mean something and everyone experiences the same emotions you want them to experience.

You've learned the different types of lenses (zoom, prime) and the different focal lengths (wide, normal, long). Now you are going to learn the different types of shots you have at your disposal for use in your composition. What do you want in each shot? You want to show what is important for that moment in the film.

CHAPTER 16

Camera Shots

On the set you have to be able to communicate your film language with the crew so that all of you are speaking the same language. If you call out a certain type of shot and it's not communicated properly then you won't get what you want. Keep your communication simple. Make sure to develop your language during pre-production before shooting begins.

Shooting is no different than writing, because each shot has an action and a reaction that follows. Hopefully your reactions are better than the actions. The smallest little gesture or eye movement can have great meaning. Too many writers/filmmakers rely on dialog to get their point across. Challenge yourself to use visuals. A look may be the most important shot you have. What isn't said can be much more interesting and important than something that is said.

3 BASIC SHOTS

The three basic shots you'll be using are the Long Shot, Medium Shot and Close Up. Each one of these shots has many variations. The shots all relate to the size of the subject (image size) in the frame or the area of concentration you want your audience to experience.

Long Shot *(LS)*

First you must realize that a long shot is not the same thing as a long lens. The long shot covers a wide area of concentration, which means the subject size is **small** compared to the rest of the frame…small compared to their surroundings in the shot. The LS is the **most basic shot** and is usually a short duration shot, often used to open a film and end a film. It is also called an establishing shot, wide shot or master shot, because it shows the audience everything of importance in a given scene: who, what, when, where and why. It helps the audience become oriented to the new scene location/surroundings. The LS shows your subjects in their surroundings. The LS establishes the area of action, shows people entering and exiting a scene and subjects moving around. To the audience the LS is the **most relaxing shot**. It decreases tension because the audience views things from a distance. They are not yet in the middle of the action nor can they hear specific dialog. The LS allows the audience to catch their breath on the roller coaster. Long Shots show small subject sizes in relation to the rest of the frame.

Clara Natoli

Medium Long Shot *(MS)*

MLS shows full body length, but not much of the surroundings. In TV it's called a Full Shot. Notice how the subject size is larger compared to the rest of the frame than in the Long Shots.

Sanjay Pindiyath

Extreme Long Shot (ELS)

The ELS is usually an exterior shot overlooking a vast landscape showing cities, mountains, prairies, etc. The ELS is best used for the opening and closing shots in epic films. The subject size is very small compared to the rest of the frame if they are present in the shot.

Clara Natoli

Medium Shot (MS) or Mid Shot

A MS shows a **larger** subject size than a LS, which means more concentration on the subject than a LS provides. It concentrates on a smaller area than a LS. The MS is the **most used shot** and focuses on a smaller group of subjects or area rather than the whole group or vast area like in the LS. The MS can show your subjects from just above the knees and up. The MS is best used for the interaction between 2 (Two-Shot) or more (Group Shot) subjects. The audience gets more involved with them. The audience feels as if they are one of the group and they are able to hear conversations and see everyone's reactions. The tension and action in the MS are increased compared to the LS. If the LS is a shot of the whole party then the MS is a small group at the party.

Anita Patterson Peppers

Close-Up Shot (CU)

The CU shows you the **largest** subject size. It is the most concentrated, **most important and most powerful shot**. The CU focuses the attention of your audience onto one single subject giving them all the details...all the secrets. The CU provides the climax of a scene by showing something significant. The CU gives your shot that knockout punch, that drama, that comedy. The tension, drama and action are at their peak. A CU emphasizes whatever you are shooting. It's like holding a magnifying glass up to your subject. The camera should be positioned level with the subject's eyes, because the **eyes are the most telling** feature of the human body. Any police officer will tell you that a person's eyes tell it all!

The truth or not the truth is all in the eyes. The CU puts the audience right in the middle of the scene. Everything else that was in the LS or the MS is now gone. There are many types of CU's. If you simply say a CU then most cinematographers would frame and shoot the head and shoulders of the subject. Following are different Close Ups. Notice how large the subject size is compared to a MS or LS.

Xenia Antunes

Anita Patterson Peppers

Medium CU: From a subject's stomach to above their head.

Head & Shoulder CU: Below their shoulders to above their head - the most used shot when shooting dialogue.

Head CU: Their head only.

Extreme CU: Their eyes, nose, mouth, or minute details of something.

Point of View (POV) CU's: Shot as if standing next to the subject.

CU's as Transition Shots: You can open a scene with a CU to give clues to that scene. A lug nut being tightened shows the scene might be taking place in an auto shop. A drink being poured might be in a bar or at a party. A gun being fired could be at a gun range or a murder taking place. The shot may lead the audience to thinking one thing or misleading them on purpose. Most films open with a LS to show the location. Mix it up and use some variety. A scene may end with a CU and then the next scene opens with a similar CU.

Let's summarize the three shots by using the party example. When someone first walks into a big party. That first moment when entering the whole party scene, that is the LS. When they move to a group of people that is the MS. When they end up talking one-on-one with someone, that is the CU.

Combining all three shots (LS, MS and CU) or two of them into one shot gives great depth to a shot. You can have one subject in CU, one in MS and one in LS all in deep focus in the same shot. Compose your shots to give the greatest depth possible.

Ken Kiser

Camera movement or subject movement can turn any shot into a different kind of shot. You may start out shooting a LS and your shot ends in a CU.

Cutting Height

Where you cut for each shot is very important. Cutting refers to where you frame your subjects.

Correct cutting heights:
- Below the shoulders
- Below the chest
- Below the waist
- Below the crotch
- Below the knees

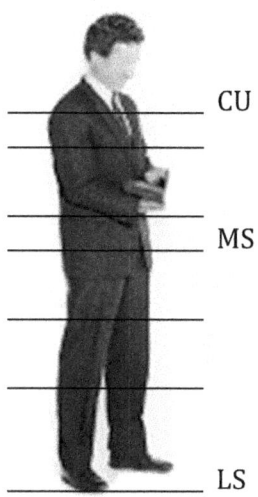

Incorrect cutting heights:
- Below the elbows but just above the wrist. If you show their wrists then show their hands.
- Below the ankles without showing the feet. If you show their ankles then show their feet.
- Don't cut through the neck, waist, knees or ankles if at all possible.

Additional Shots

Coverage *(Protection Shots)*

These are extra shots from extra angles. It is important to shoot coverage in case your intended shots don't work. It's the same as buying insurance. You hope you don't need it, but when you do it's invaluable. Coverage provides additional shots for editing. CU reaction shots are one of the best shots to use for coverage. Anytime you're shooting and having a difficult time on certain shots make sure you shoot coverage. Try something different and be inventive. Make sure you shoot coverage for long duration shots in case the shots are too long or some part of the shot doesn't work the way you intended. Coverage gives you a means for shortening shot duration by cutting long portions of a shot and inserting a shorter coverage shot. Coverage also allows you to lengthen shot duration by adding in coverage shots. Coverage is a key tool to use for pacing in your film.

Inserts

Often a CU of a subject, but usually not a character that is part of the scene.

Cut-In

CU of part of the main action taking place at that moment in the scene.

Cut-Away

A shot away from the main action, but still relevant to the main action. Cut-aways have many uses such as to divert the audience's attention to something happening elsewhere, especially when the main action is too much to stomach. The sight of a needle being injected into someone's arm still makes most audience members squirm and they thank filmmakers for a cut-in or cut-away in those cases. Cut-aways are often used to symbolize what is happening. You might use a tiger pacing back and forth to represent the Main Character in prison...losing their mind at being caged up. A shot of a sandwich being eaten may represent lunch or a time of relaxation. Weapons being loaded may open a scene of war or violence to follow. Cut-aways are used as coverage in editing. They are great for covering up shooting mistakes. Add them to your shot list for every scene.

It's better to cut-in than to cut-away from the main action, because you're not breaking the main action flow of the scene.

Reaction Shot

CU's showing the subject's response to the action or to another subject. These are great coverage shots and are shot without dialog and are **MOS**. MOS means it is shot without recording sound. The supposed MOS definition originated when a German director tried pronouncing "without sound" and it came out as "mit out sound (sprechen)." Hence MOS!

Two-shot *(2-shot)*

Two subjects together, usually shot from the waist up. If you see both of their faces or the back side of their heads it is a MS.

Anita Patterson Peppers

Group Shot

More than two subjects in one shot. Either a LS or MS.

Phaedra Wilkinson

Shot/Reverse Shot *or* Over-the-Shoulder Shot

CU's, that show only the head and shoulders of the two subjects or MS's that show more. Overlap the subjects so you see the back of the foreground subject's head, their one shoulder, maybe the side of their face, but not their nose. If you see the foreground person's nose it is considered a 2-shot. These shots are normally used for dialogue between two or more subjects. Depending on how close the subjects are together you would use over-the-shoulder shots or single CU's of them talking.

Phaedra Wilkinson   *Clara Natoli*

Matching Eye-lines

When you shoot separate shots of two or more subjects talking or looking at each other you have to match their eye-lines. Make sure their eye-lines are shot so it appears to the audience that these two subjects are looking at each other. If one subject is looking off camera and the other is looking almost directly at the camera it may appear to the audience that they are not looking at each other. Also if the two subjects

CAMERA SHOTS

are the same height and both subjects are looking down or up it wouldn't appear as if they were looking at each other. Framing subjects looking to the right and left is easy compared to framing subjects more straight on who are looking near the camera or up or down in relation to the camera. For example, a parent talking to their child where the parent is looking down at the child. The parent would look down below the camera lens and to the side while the child would look up above the camera lens and to the side.

Pick-up Shot

It is a shot to correct a portion of a shot that was not performed correctly, had technical problems (camera/sound), or may simply be a portion of a shot that the director wants done in another way. You are re-shooting only a portion of that shot.

Point Of View (POV)

There is much discussion on what is meant by a POV shot and what the different types of POV shots include. You can develop your own definition, but make sure your cast and crew know what you are trying to achieve. A POV shot refers to how intimate the audience gets with the subjects in the shot...meaning the audience feels as if they are actually part of/in the film.

An **Objective** POV shot means the audience sees the subject and also sees what the subject is seeing, all in one shot...all in the same frame. Everything is happening in front of the audience in this one shot. You don't see the subject and what the subject is looking at in separate shots. In this POV shot the audience is not part of the shot nor do they take part in the shot. Manipulation of the audience is less than in other types of POV shots.

A **Partially Objective/Subjective** POV shot means the audience sees the subject in one shot and sees what the subject is looking at in a different shot. Usually the subject's face is shown in one shot, which sets up the audience by getting them to identify with the subject. Then the next shot shows what the subject is looking at. This allows the filmmaker to impart their thoughts onto the audience and generate an emotion out of them. It's as if the audience is standing next to the subject in the shot and almost looking through their eyes. Shooting and editing of the shots develops a meaning to manipulate the emotions of the audience. You the filmmaker decide how the audience should feel. Some people will call this an objective shot and some will call it a subjective shot. To some people objective means that you aren't seeing things exactly from the subject's eyes. Call it whatever you like. It is not a 100% objective or subjective shot.

A **Subjective** POV shot would be where the audience is actually looking through the subject's eyes and sees everything the subject sees as if they were the subject in the film. Other subjects in the film talk and look directly into the camera…directly at the audience. Newscasters and commercials use subjective shots and talk directly to the audience at home. Narration in a film makes the audience part of the cast, because the narration is directed at them not anyone in the film. If you want the audience to feel what the subject is feeling, such as intoxicated, hallucinating, dizzy, spinning out of control, scared, etc. you can use subjective shots.

Let's use a horror film as a way to explain POV shots. An objective POV shot would show the killer stalking their victim all in one shot. You see how the killer and victim react to each other all in the one shot. No manipulating the audience with other shots. No cutting away from that shot. A partially objective/subjective shot would show the killer, then show the victim's reaction to the killer as the killer stalks them. The victim would be looking at the killer, not at the camera. A subjective shot would mean the audience is the killer. The audience would be looking through their eyes as they stalk the victim and the victim looks right back into the camera as if the audience is the killer. Understand? This type of subjective shooting is not done very often. *Ferris Bueller's Day Off* included subjective shots where he talked directly to the camera, which meant he was talking directly to the audience as if they were part of the film.

Objective: You watch the subject and the action.

Partially: You are standing next to the subject and you are part of the action.

Subjective: You are the subject and the action.

CAMERA SHOTS 115

Exercise: *Analyze footage of your favorite films with the sound off. Name the types of shots as they appear on the screen. LS, MS, CU and all of their variations. You can break down any shot in any film. Are the POV shots objective or subjective? It may be tough to tell exactly whether the lens is a wide, normal or long lens, but you can come close to recognizing the exact lens that was used. The key is to understand what each lens represents and more importantly to know how to use the LS, MS and CU to get what you want.*

The next chapter describes how to start building your puzzle by focusing on how each shot fits together into the scenes, sequences, acts and the finished film. Prior to this point you have been focusing only on the individual shots by themselves.

CHAPTER **17**

Shooting Techniques

There are several shooting techniques used by filmmakers. A shooting technique is simply the way you shoot and edit your shots in order.

Standard Shooting Technique
(Master Scene Technique/Progressive Shooting)

The number one method for shooting **scenes** is called the Standard Shooting Technique where the LS is shot first, then the MS and then the CU. This also refers to the way the film is edited. The LS comes first, then the MS then the CU. You start with a small subject size in a large area (LS) then move to a larger subject in a smaller area (MS) and end with the largest subject filling the frame (CU). The subject size increases as the scene goes from shot to shot. Does this mean every scene needs to start off with a LS and end with a CU? No! Nor does every scene need to have all of these shots or variations of these shots.

In this series of shots the subject, or Center of Interest, increases in size. The LS captures the whole scene if necessary. This shows the audience where they are and what is in the scene. They would not see the detail, but they would know the setting. The MS brings the audience closer to the action. Then of course the audience is right in the middle of the action when they get to the CU.

LS → **MS** → **CU**
Beginning   Middle   Climax/End

Everything moves **in** closer and closer to the subject, focusing the audience's attention on the subject. The action, tension, pacing and drama increase as you move in closer. The standard shooting technique follows the way people are in normal life, because people love to see what's going on and get closer to the action. If you have seen a fire or an auto accident, you know people want to get a closer look. It is human nature. The Standard Shooting Technique is just that, moving in for a closer look. It focuses the audience's attention from the overall scene (LS) to the group of people (MS) to the individual (CU).

As you move from LS to MS to CU you want to narrow the eye-line or horizontal camera angle in line with the eyes/face of the subject. This changing of camera angles is known as the "**30 Degree Rule**" and will be discussed in detail in the next chapter. Each shot gets closer in line with the subject's eyes as you move in closer and the subject size increases. The audience gets more intimate the more in line they are with a subject's eyes. Remember, the eyes tell the story. The audience feels they are as close as they can get to being a part of the story, without actually being spoken to directly. So not only should you change the subject size between shots, you need to change camera angles as well.

The "30 Degree Rule" only refers to the horizontal camera angle. The vertical camera angle should also change. As you move to the CU you want to get closer to being at the same height as the subject. Start out higher (most of the time) or lower than the subject in the LS then move in closer for the MS and then right at the subject's eyes for the CU.

If you were to edit directly from a LS to a CU it's an even more intense, shocking effect, because it happens so fast. It draws immediate attention to it. Remember when shooting the LS that you don't want to be straight in line (think angles) with the subject, since your CU will be as close to being straight in line with the subject as possible. You are moving from basic information to focused, detailed information when moving from a LS to a CU. The faster you go from LS to CU, the faster the action for the audience.

SHOOTING TECHNIQUES

Shots are usually shot out of sequence, but the main reason to shoot the LS first is because it's easier to match lighting going from the big shot setup (LS) to the small shot (CU) setup. Everything can be scaled down: the cast, the crew, the extras, the lighting. You can save time and money by shooting only the beginning and ending of any LS instead of shooting the whole scene. If you know you will edit the middle portion of the LS with other shots then why waste the time and money?

Now it stands to reason that you also have a **Non-Standard Shooting Technique**, which is the opposite of the standard shooting technique. In this case the subject size decreases as the scene goes from CU to MS to LS.

Non-Standard Shooting Technique
(Regressive Shooting)

Start shooting/editing with the CU's first and then move to the MS and then to the LS. This technique is sometimes used to open up a scene with a CU and then pull back to reveal the larger scene all in one shot. Horror/thriller films might start with a CU of the victim or the killer. *Bonnie and Clyde* used this technique throughout the film with great impact.

CU →	**MS** →	**LS**
Beginning	Middle	End

As you move from CU to MS to LS you move from a large subject size to a smaller one. The action, tension, pacing and drama decrease. You are moving **out** to re-establish the over-all scene. The drama has decreased and now you can move on happily ever after or you might be adding in new subjects or new events about to happen. You want to do the opposite with the horizontal and vertical camera angles as you move out. You want to move further out of alignment with the subject's eyes and raise the camera or on occasion lower it. Most of the time you will raise the height of the camera as you move out from CU to MS to LS.

Two additional shot selection techniques and editing techniques are Contrast and Repetitive Shooting/Editing.

Contrast Shooting/Editing

Contrast shooting/editing means you shoot/edit different subject sizes in sequence such as a CU and LS together or you have contrasting images: winners and losers, the calm and the storm, rich and poor, strong and weak, old and young. The subject size should change dramatically, not a slight change, when shooting/editing different subject sizes. You can mix both the subject size difference and contrasting images together to increase the impact.

Repetitive Shooting/Editing

Repetitive shooting/editing means you shoot/edit a series of shots of the same subject size, same look, and/or related images. The distance from the subject should also remain the same. They could be CU's showing character's reactions, LS's of buildings, MS's of bugs, CU's of wealth, etc.

These four basic techniques should help you understand how to build a scene/sequence of shots. For each scene ask yourself whether you want rising tension, rising drama, rising action and quicker pacing? If so use the standard technique. Or do you want everything to decrease by using the non-standard technique. Or do you want the tension, drama, pacing and action to stay at the same levels? Use the contrast and/or repetition techniques. Now you can see why you need to know how you will edit your film in order to determine the shots you will need to make each scene impact the audience.

As a filmmaker you want to keep your film interesting to your audience by varying your shots and sequences. Your audience wants variety.

Exercise: *Analyze footage from your favorite films to see how scenes are pieced together. Are the subject sizes going from larger to smaller (CU to MS to LS) as the shots are edited together? Are they going from smaller to larger (LS to MS to CU)? Are they jumping back and forth from larger to smaller, then smaller to larger? You will notice how the angles change between shots. Angles will be covered in the next chapter. Take note which technique is used the most throughout each film. How often do you see*

SHOOTING TECHNIQUES

standard, non-standard, contrast and repetitive shooting/editing? Do the tension, drama, pacing and action rise, fall or remain the same? A good roller coaster gives you just enough time to catch your breath before it takes your breath away again. Up and down and around you go again and again. Shoot and edit several scenes using the different techniques discussed in this chapter. Use scenes from one of your favorite scripts, find a few friends to act them out and shoot them. You have to practice shooting and editing footage using the techniques discussed.

Review Time

At this point it's time for a quick review of the last few sections/chapters. You now know that there are three sizes of lenses: wide, normal and long and three types of shots: LS, MS and CU. Many filmmakers confuse the shots with the lenses. Don't think you have to use a wide lens for a LS or a wide lens for a CU or any shot. You must determine what you want to show in each frame. Your LS could be done with a wide, normal or long lens and the same for your MS and CU. Your lens sizes determine your depth of field and the look of your shots. This is why filmmaking is all about experimenting, practicing and making films so you know how to make the right choices.

CHAPTER **18**

Camera Angles

Now you'll learn how camera angles impact your audience. Where you physically place the camera for each shot is extremely important. Some people simply set the camera in a certain spot without knowing why they put it in that spot. If someone were to ask you why you placed the camera where you did then you should be able to give them an answer.

Think in terms of angles. Think 3-D. Angles add depth and dimension to each shot. A 45 degree angle gives you the most depth and dimension. Shooting straight on a subject, with no angle, gives you the least amount of depth and dimension causing your shots to look flat. That high school trigonometry keeps coming back to haunt you. Place the camera at angles to a subject rather than straight on a subject. For example if you were looking straight at a box you would only see one side and it would simply look like a flat piece of cardboard. Once you move above or below the box and to the side you see three sides...three dimensions.

Each time you shoot a new shot of a scene; change the subject size in the frame (LS, MS, CU) as well as the vertical and horizontal camera angles in relation to your subject. It is called **Angle Plus Angle** shooting. It is the best and only way you should shoot. The camera is angled in both the vertical plane and the horizontal plane in relation to your subject. It makes for a professional looking film.

Luis Tejo

Vertical Camera Angle

The vertical camera angle refers to whether the camera is above, below, level with or tilted towards the subject. The camera doesn't have to be extremely high or low, just enough to show the depth and dimension. The impact on the audience depends on which angle you use.

Level: Placing the camera level with the subject, at their eye level, is a neutral shot. It doesn't add any extra emotion or drama to the scene like a high or low angle shot. Your audience feels things are normal.

High Angle: Placing the camera above your subject and pointing down on them diminishes them. It makes the audience feel superior looking down on this poor soul. The subject is in an inferior position not in a position of importance. It shows them as the worker bee not the boss. It's a great shot to show the subject as weak, insignificant, downtrodden, unimportant or down on their luck.

Anita Patterson Peppers   *Clara Natoli*

Low Angle: Placing the camera lower than the subject and pointing up at them shows the subject as powerful, important, menacing. It adds tension and drama. The audience feels weak looking up at this powerful person. The subject is the boss! It puts them up on a pedestal. Have you ever looked up at the Empire State building, Eiffel Tower, Arch or other tall structure? It makes you feel very inferior. It makes you dizzy. It adds drama. The judge in a courtroom always sits higher than everyone else. The judge is god in that courtroom. Your audience will identify with the lowly subject looking up at this higher power. *The Wizard of Oz* was the almighty power. *Citizen Kane* used low angles for when Kane was a young and dominant figure. It also used low angles when he was old and weak, but in this case the room plays the dominant figure. It overpowers him in his old age showing his loneliness and isolation.

Scott Liddell   *P. Winberg*

Let's use a bowling ball as another example. If it's sitting down below us we're not afraid of it. If it's sitting up on a shelf above us we fear it, because it has the potential to roll off the shelf and smash us on the head. A large boulder sitting up on a ledge gives us the same feeling.

Now you know how the three vertical camera angles impact your audience. For each shot you shoot you have to use one of the three vertical angles. Know what feelings or emotions you are trying to get out of your audience. Then shoot accordingly. Think angles!

Dutch Camera Angle *(Oblique Angle)*

If you place the camera in a vertically tilted manner so there are no vertical lines and no level horizon, you impact the audience by making them feel off balance and unstable. You give them a disorienting feeling. People want things to be level and balanced. Use these shots for confusion, tension, disorientation, disaster or to show a subject that is unbalanced. These shots usually look best when shot from a low angle in addition to the Dutch angle. Following are Dutch angle shots.

Anita Patterson Peppers

Keith Richardson

If the image tilts to the right it carries more weight and is more forceful looking than the image tilting to the left. If you show the horizon tilting down from left to right it gives the audience a feeling of going downhill. If you show the horizon tilting up from left to right it gives the audience a feeling of going uphill.

CAMERA ANGLES

Horizontal Camera Angle *(30 Degree Rule, 45 Degree Rule)*

When shooting shots within the same scene you should shoot each shot at least 30 degrees off an axis drawn from the previous shot. If you simply move the camera along the same line towards your subject then the shots will have a leapfrog effect (jump cut) from one shot to the next. You don't want to jump from shot to shot along the same line towards the subject, unless that is what you intend to do. It disorients the audience.

As you move in closer to your subject (LS to MS to CU), move more in-line with your subject's eyes...LS to MS to CU...large angle to medium angle to small angle with respect to your subject's eyes.

As you move out away from your subject (CU to MS to LS), move more out-of-line with your subject's eyes...CU to MS to LS...small angle to medium angle to large angle with respect to your subject's eyes. One way to eliminate having to use the rule is to drastically change the subject size such as shooting/editing a LS to an Extreme CU. This subject size difference eliminates the jump cut look of cutting two similar sized images from the exact same angle.

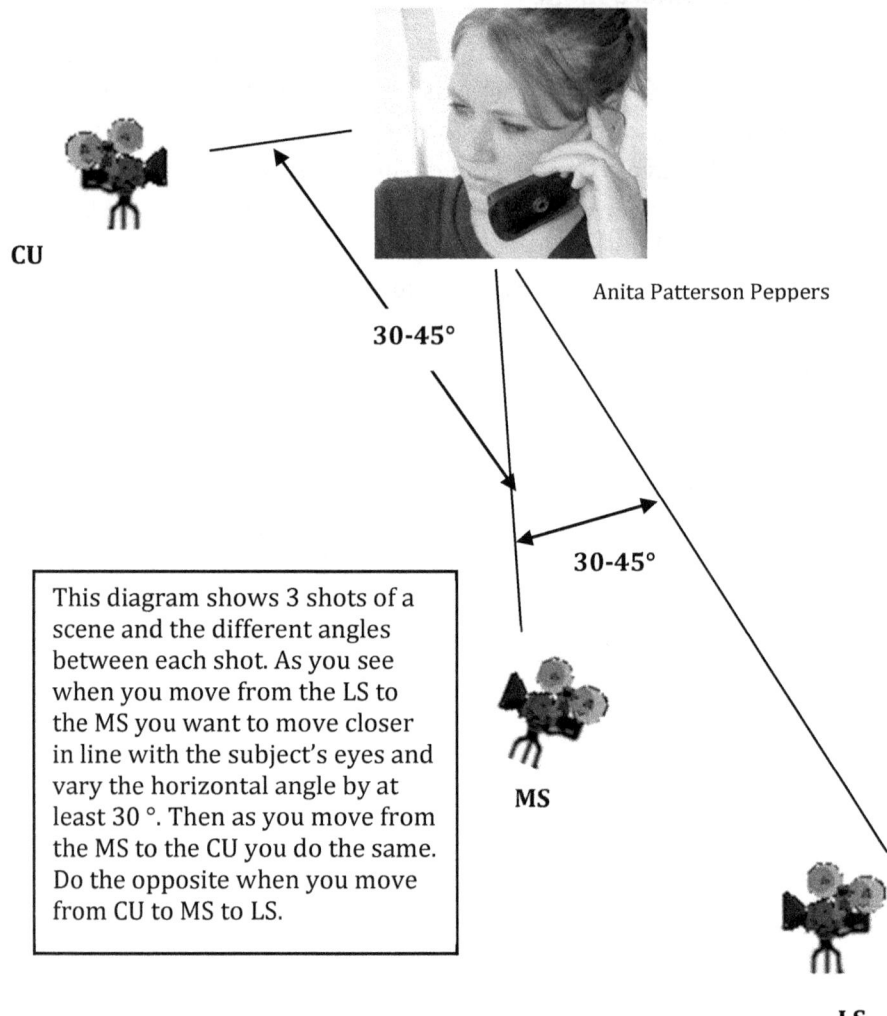

Anita Patterson Peppers

This diagram shows 3 shots of a scene and the different angles between each shot. As you see when you move from the LS to the MS you want to move closer in line with the subject's eyes and vary the horizontal angle by at least 30 °. Then as you move from the MS to the CU you do the same. Do the opposite when you move from CU to MS to LS.

Most films shoot/edit from a LS to a CU and change the horizontal angle almost 90 degrees. A LS from the side and a CU almost directly in front of the subject. This is very common in scenes with subject movement such as a subject driving or walking.

CAMERA ANGLES

*__Exercise__: Analyze footage from your favorite films and notice how the camera angles (Vertical, Dutch, Horizontal) and subject sizes (LS, MS, CU) change between shots/cuts. Make note of the impact it has on you when you see the different shots. Look for shots within the same scene to see where the angle **and** the subject size do not change. Very rarely will you ever find this to be the case. It is not a natural or balanced method of shooting. Shoot footage using different angles and subject sizes and analyze your footage.*

CHAPTER **19**

Camera & Subject Movement

You will be shooting static camera shots (non-moving) and moving camera shots, static subjects and moving subjects and every combination you can imagine. You must know how to compose your shots when incorporating movement. Remember that simply moving the camera doesn't mean action and increased pacing for a shot. Movement must aid in telling your story by showing something new. Don't use movement just to use movement. The reason most filmmakers use movement is because everybody else uses movement. Don't jump into the lake just because everybody else is jumping into the lake. You have to move the camera with a purpose in mind. The moves have to be logical and not distract the audience. It's usually easier to move the subject rather than the camera. If you move the camera, subject or both, do so because it reveals additional information which the audience would not have without the movement.

Try to move subjects toward or away from the camera at angles (diagonally) rather than straight at or away from the camera or straight across the screen. This adds a feeling of depth to your film. **Move at angles and shoot at angles.** Add depth to your shots by having your subjects move in between other actors, props, furniture, etc. Always improve the story by asking yourself, "How can I make this more interesting?"

Camera movement can often be used in place of several static shots to follow the same action, but remember if you only shoot one long shot of a scene it better be a shot you will use from beginning to end. If you don't have additional shots to use during editing then you are stuck with this one long shot. So remember to shoot coverage. Coverage allows you to adjust the pacing and get in or out of a scene quicker or later than you might have first thought. Coverage allows you to edit out any portion of a shot that doesn't work.

Even if you have movement in a shot, start each shot with a static camera and a static subject and end with the same unless the subject exits out of the frame. Most cinematographers would shoot the shot with the camera movement coming to a stop before the subject exits the frame. Experiment and practice.

As you move the camera, subject or both, your subject size, angles and focus may be changing as your movement takes place. Always anticipate your subject movement prior to your subject actually moving. This means the camera should start moving in the same direction as your subject, but just prior to them moving.

Types of Camera Movement

Camera movement allows you to show more than can be viewed with a static shot, because you are covering more area. You can show more of the scene setting, reveal new information and follow the action.

Following are different methods of moving the camera.

Dolly

A wheeled support for the camera. Low budget filmmakers often use wheelchairs, skateboards or their car to follow subject movement. For smooth camera shots on rough surfaces, dollies can be run on track laid down over the rough surface.

Handheld

Use a wide lens for handheld shooting, because the wider the lens the smoother the movement and the steadier the shot will be. A long lens is nearly impossible to hold steady. Use a wide lens unless you want a shaky shot. Don't use a handheld camera just to make the shots look shaky unless you have a good reason. What is your reason for making the audience get motion sickness? You might have to sell motion sickness medicine at the concession stand.

Steadicam/Body Mounts

An apparatus supported by the body of the camera operator. The shots are very similar to hand-held, but much smoother, because the steadicam has a built-in stabilizer.

Car Mount, Plane, Helicopter, Remote Vehicle

The camera is attached to a vehicle using a mounting fixture.

Crane/Boom

The camera is attached to a crane or boom that allows the camera to start in any number of positions and end up in another position...such as starting at ground level and reaching heights of several hundred feet.

Pan

Panning is side-to-side camera rotation in the horizontal plane from left to right or right to left. You rotate the camera on its support, which is usually a tripod.

Cross Pan

A panning shot that follows one subject going one direction then another coming from the opposite direction. The cross pan switches from one direction to the opposite direction.

Swish Pan

A pan that moves fast enough to blur the image. Sometimes used as a transition between scenes without actually cutting to another shot.

Tilt

Tilting is an up or down camera rotation in the vertical plane on its support, which is usually a tripod or crane. A tilt is also called a vertical pan.

Tracking

Tracking is where you follow the subject as they move. Most often the camera is supported on a dolly or a steadicam.

Counter Move

The camera and subject move in opposite directions. The camera moves one way, but pans to follow the subject moving the opposite way.

Shoot short camera moving shots. Straight cuts are always faster than moving shots. Straight cuts get to the point of a scene quicker. Moving shots of static action tend to slow things down rather than speeding them up. It does just the opposite of what most people think. When you have a lengthy action/movement such as a long driving shot or person walking make sure to provide additional angles or coverage to allow the shot to be cut. Coverage, coverage, coverage! You don't want to have to go back out on location and re-shoot after you've wrapped the production and are knee-deep in the editing phase. Don't shoot your way into a bad editing process. Plan for problems.

A note about using a tripod. Always point one leg of the tripod in the direction of your lens when shooting. That way your tripod will not tip over in that direction and land directly on your lens. If your tripod is going to tip or fall you want it coming towards you or to the side. You shouldn't ever transport your camera while it's mounted on your tripod. I know people will lift and move the tripod and camera while they are attached so if you do you must be sure to lift by the tripod only. Do not lift by the camera. You can damage your lens mounting flange and/or your camera body if you pick up your camera including the tripod weight.

Types of Subject Movement

The audience thinks about subject movement in regards to our sense of direction, which is north, south, east and west.

North

Subject moves across the frame from the lower left to upper right.

South

Subject moves across the frame from the upper right to lower left.

East

Subject moves across the frame from left to right.

West

Subject moves across the frame from right to left.

Back & Forth

Pacing like a caged animal or a clock pendulum, induces a claustrophobic, helpless feeling, boredom, monotony, a prison cell, anxiety, a subject losing their mind.

Changing Directions

Moving in more than one direction and at angles is always best for the audience. It gives the audience more to watch.

Circles

Moving in a circle induces a fun, happy feeling in the audience like an amusement park ride.

Curved

Serpentine movement like a snake suggests trouble, mystery, covert action, secretive, undetected, comedy in the right situation.

Diagonal Movement

Gives the audience the strongest feelings, especially if you have two subjects going towards each other, one going Up from Left to Right and the other coming Down from Right to Left. A battle of good versus evil is taking place. Mountain climbers always seem to be climbing lower left to upper right facing the challenge, then coming back down off the mountain from upper right to lower left. Back to reality.

Horizontal

As your subject moves horizontally it gives the audience a feeling of travel, someone/something on the move, moving on to the next thing whether it's good or bad. For anyone who reads left to right, such as in the U.S., a subject moving from Left to Right seems more at ease, more fluid and is easiest for the audience to follow. Moving from Right to Left is just the opposite. It also shows the power position. If your villain is going from Left to Right then your Main Character should be going from Right to Left.

Vertical

Upward movement in the frame from bottom to top gives the audience an uplifting feeling, freedom, flying away, newness, religious, rising above everyone else stuck in the muck. Downward movement in the frame from top to bottom gives the feeling of coming back down to earth, back to reality, time for a showdown, drama, the time of reckoning has come, possible doom and gloom.

Exercise: Analyze footage from your favorite films for different camera moves. See how they reveal additional information in each shot in regards to character, space, setting, time, action and story. Take your camera and try your own camera moves. Pay particular attention to the speed of your camera movement. Moving too fast can blur the image. Moving too slow can waste too much screen time. Find a subject so you can practice pans, tilts, and handheld camera moves.

Analyze footage from your favorite films for subject movement and take note of the impact it has on you. What if any feelings do you feel? Make note of all the different types of directional movement you see.

CHAPTER 20

Balance

Balance means balancing your subjects in your film frame. For the audience it is the same as having balance in their life. The audience looks for balance, visually (physically) and mentally. If you want to knock the audience off balance, show them an unbalanced frame. Unbalanced frames show us a world where something is wrong. If you have an unbalanced shot, but intended to have a balanced shot, the audience may miss what you were trying to achieve. If your goal is to make the audience feel off balance, confused, uncomfortable or tense then do it.

Rule of Thirds

The Rule of Thirds is the most widely used and most basic fundamental in shooting. If you don't learn anything other than this then you will still be in great shape! Most films hold up to this rule. There might be a few exceptions, but very few.

The rule of thirds is simple: divide the film frame into thirds both vertically and horizontally by adding four imaginary lines: two vertical and two horizontal. This divides your frame into equal parts. When you look through your camera eyepiece you have to imagine those lines are there in your frame in order to balance the frame.

Anita Patterson Peppers

Phaedra Wilkinson

Once you visually divide your frame then you can position your subjects in the proper places:

- Place the key subjects in the frame at the intersections of the axes.
- Place your subject's eyes on the top horizontal line (axis) so you don't leave too much headroom in the frame. For an Extreme CU the eyes would still be positioned on the top horizontal line even though the subject's head is out of the frame.
- Place your subject's nose ½ way up in the frame for CU's. The subject's eyes may be at or near the top horizontal line as well.
- Place the horizon (exterior shots) on the top horizontal line or the bottom horizontal line not ½ way up or down in the frame. Some of your horizon decisions also depend on additional subjects you have in the frame. Change your shots around. In one shot you could place the horizon on the lower horizontal line of the frame and in another shot the horizon could be placed on the top horizontal line of the frame.
- Try not to divide the frame in ½ in any direction: diagonally, vertically or horizontally. You can place huge subjects (mountains, skyscrapers, valleys, etc.) in the middle of the frame or a tree with branches coming out in all directions. None of these will give the audience the feeling of an unbalanced frame. If you put a mountain or overpowering subject on one side of the frame it feels as if the frame might tip over. You would need to balance the frame.
- Try to place subjects on the vertical lines not in the middle of the frame. If a subject is looking to the right then you would place

them on the left side vertical line. If a subject is looking to the left then place them on the right side vertical line. This leaves open space in the direction they are looking.
- The right side of the frame is stronger so you can place a larger subject on the left side than on the right and the frame will still appear balanced.

The following shots show proper placement of subjects.

Luis Tejo

Anita Patterson Peppers

Luis Tejo

Xenia Antunes

As movement of the subject or camera occurs within the frame, you need to readjust your framing to keep it balanced. You balance on the move.

Frame-Within-a-Frame

Add to your shots by framing your subjects using props or building frames. You might position your subject in a door frame or between trees or anything that frames them up. Don't let the frame become the Center of Interest for the shot. It's best to shoot at angles so the frame and subject are not two-dimensional. This will help separate the subject from the frame.

Keith Richardson   *Anita Patterson Peppers*

If your frame is equal on both sides it gives the audience a balanced feeling: everything is at peace, everything is good, no problems, no conflict. If it's not equal and balanced then your audience has the opposite feeling. Use these balancing decisions to your advantage to impact your audience.

<u>Exercise</u>: Tape thin strips of paper across your TV screen or whatever you are watching your films on…two horizontally and two vertically, dividing the screen into thirds in each direction. Do not put tape on the screen itself. Analyze footage of your favorite films. Notice where the eyeline and nose of your subjects are positioned in the frame. Notice how the subjects are on one vertical line or the other, depending on which way they are looking or moving. Notice where subjects are positioned when looking/moving one direction or another to see if a portion of the screen frame is open in the direction they are looking. Look for horizons and notice where they are framed. How does the frame shift during movement of the subject, camera or both? Remember, to turn off the sound when viewing footage to focus on the visuals.

Proper positioning of subjects within the frame allows the filmmaker to balance the frame, but how do you direct the audience's attention to the right spot in your shot, which is called the Center of Interest?

CHAPTER **21**

Center of Interest

To grab the audience's attention you must direct them to look at your Center of Interest by making it stand out in the frame. Here are the many ways to direct the audience's attention:

Moving

Moving subjects always stand out compared to a static subject.

Larger

The largest subject always gets more attention. If several subjects are moving then the subject moving towards the camera stands out the most, because the subject size gets larger as the subject comes closer to the camera and thus closer to the audience.

Brightness

Brighter light, colors, clothing stand out more than dark areas, colors or clothing.

Higher in Frame

The highest subject usually stands out more than any subjects in the lower part of the frame, because the higher position is the power position. The Preacher stands while the congregation sits.

Right Side

The right side of the frame is always stronger. If the frame is balanced in regards to color, light, movement, etc. then the audience's eyes automatically move to the right side of the frame.

If you can't place the subject on the right side of the frame then you will have to make the subject stand out in another fashion such as any of these other choices.

Sound

Sound/noise always draws more attention. If someone is talking while others are listening then the audience's attention is naturally drawn to the speaker.

Single

A single subject stands out from a group. The group blends together while the lone subject stands out. Ever notice at a party who stands out? The single person. A rebel leader standing out amongst followers. The lone tree or lone wolf!

In Focus

If you shift the focus from one subject to another. The audience always looks for the subject or area that is most in focus. Shift the focus to the area where you want the audience to look. If you shift the focus then you shift the audience's attention. For example, you might have a scene where one person is talking to several people and you see another figure in the background, but it is out of focus. Your attention is on the person talking because they are in focus. Maybe the person calls their boss an idiot and suddenly the focus shifts to the person in the background and guess who? It's the boss.

CENTER OF INTEREST

If you combine any of the above then you direct the audience's attention even more to the Center of Interest. For example, you dress the subject in bright clothing, move them towards the camera, into an area with more light, on the right side of the frame and bring them into clear focus.

Exercise: *Analyze footage of your favorite films to determine the Center of Interest in each shot. Determine which methods they use for directing the audience to look at the Center of Interest.*

Continuity

Continuity allows all of your shots to be edited together. Remember, a film is just a bunch of shots...a bunch of shots of a character's journey or life and only shots of the exciting parts. The boring parts are not included. Your shots have to fit together with a smooth continuous flow from one shot to the next so they fit the finished puzzle. You can take 90 years of someone's life and show it in 2 hours of **reel** time, otherwise known as screen time. If you shot it in real time it would be 90 years long. You must be able to shoot your shots so the audience understands the meaning even though you skipped around. Their imagination fills the gaps between the shots if you've given them enough information. It all must appear continuous to the audience. You can move back and forth in time and space, but in so doing you have to keep moving the story forward. Even reality shows don't show real time.

Continuity errors show up in small, low-budget films as well as huge studio event films and the reasons are many. One big reason is that most films are not shot from beginning to end. They are shot out of sequence. Keeping proper notes of what was shot three months ago so it will match up with what you will shoot tomorrow is extremely important. If your subject is wearing a blue shirt in one scene and a red shirt in the next, then you have lost continuity if they should be wearing the same shirt in both scenes. How many films have you seen where it is supposed to be raining, but you see a clear blue sky in the background? If it's supposed to be raining then don't show a clear blue sky. Frame your shots so the sky is not in the shots. If your subject has long hair in the beginning of the film and short hair in the end you have to plan for that. You would hate to find out your character still has long hair in the final shots, which were actually shot at the beginning of production. Continuity is lost. Take any film with a car chase and slow it down so you can watch it frame by frame. You will be able to see the stunt drivers up close and personal. Watch the film at normal speed and it hides the fact that someone else is doing those stunts. That allows them to keep continuity.

Keep track of each shot and the props, sets, costumes/wardrobe, hair color, hair style, lighting, make-up, etc., used in each shot. Keep track of the actions performed by a subject while delivering dialog. For example, your subject says one line then sits down in a chair, and then finishes their lines. If you shoot several different shots of this same dialog remember that the subject said one line before sitting down, and then finished their lines. It's easy to have continuity errors in your film. If you have to come back and do re-shoots at a later time these notes will be priceless. Everything must match up with the shots that were previously filmed. The **Script Supervisor** keeps track of many of these details in their script notes.

Below are common Lack-of-Continuity Examples.
- Wardrobe errors - subject wears a watch in one shot and forgets to wear it in the next shot.
- Props missing from shots.
- A burning candle is 3 inches tall in one shot and in the next shot it is 8 inches tall. Cigarettes, fires, ice or anything that changes size over time falls into the same category.
- Clocks are hard to keep correct from shot to shot.
- A period film set in the 1920's and the Stealth Bomber flies by in the background.
- Weather related errors in exterior shots - rain shots with the sun shining and a clear blue sky.
- Subject positioning is not correct from one shot to the next.
- Action not matching up from one shot to the next.
- Crossing the line during scenes…violates the 180 Degree Rule. (discussed in the next chapter)
- Lighting doesn't match from shot to shot.

CHAPTER **22**

180° Rule of Continuity

The Golden Rule of Continuity is the 180 Degree Rule! Using this rule allows you to keep continuity between all shots within a scene.

The best way to describe the 180° Rule is this: what is on the right side of the frame stays on the right and what is on the left stays on the left for every shot within a scene unless camera or subject movement causes repositioning. Draw an imaginary circle around the area you are shooting in your shot. Then draw an imaginary line dissecting the circle. This line is called the **line of action**, because it runs directly through the action in the scene. To keep continuity in a particular scene you want to shoot all of your shots from one side of the line or the other. If you remember a circle has 360° and so half a circle has 180°. There's that high school math again. Essentially, you position the camera within the 180° on one side of the line. So remember where subjects were positioned from one shot to the next.

To follow the 180° Rule, you first have to determine where the line of action is located. The best way to determine the line of action is by the direction of subject movement or the line of sight of a subject or subjects. For two football or soccer teams at opposite ends of a field the line is drawn from one team to the opposing team. During the game the cameras stay on one side of the field for all shots. If a subject is moving then the line is the drawn from the subject in the direction they are moving. If two subjects are talking then the line of action is drawn from one subject to the next.

The following diagram shows the line of action between two subjects talking.

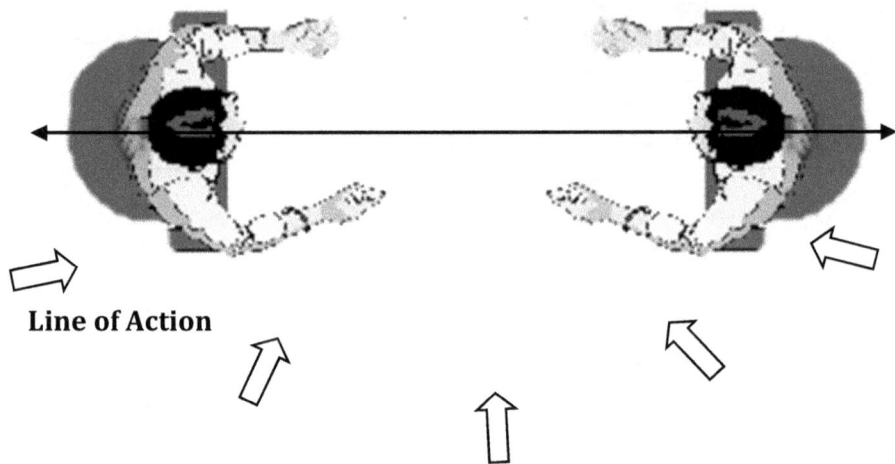

Line of Action

The Camera should stay on one side of the line or the other for all shots!

Once you have established the side of the line you will be shooting from there are ways of shooting from the opposite side. You can shoot from the opposite side of the line of action if you follow a subject crossing the line. A subject can also change the line of action by looking in another direction. If one of the subjects in the above example were to look to the left or right you can draw a new line of action in that direction. You can also move the camera across the line during the shot so that the audience sees the crossing of the line. During the edit the entire shot and camera movement need to be used in order to show the line crossing. This moves the view of the subjects from one side to the other.

Another way to change the line of action is to shoot the subject straight on or from behind. This is called a **Neutral Shot** because it is neutral as far as the line of action and direction of movement. A neutral shot has no screen direction other than towards or away from the camera and allows you to then shoot/edit the subject going in any direction after the neutral shot. A neutral shot allows you to change screen direction whenever you need to and allows you to shoot shots from the opposite side of the line of action. Always shoot a few neutral shots so you can correct any shooting errors during editing. These neutral shots are considered coverage. The shots would be labeled as **tail-away** or **head-on** neutral shots on your shot list.

Phaedra Wilkinson *Anita Patterson Peppers*

Maybe your goal is to confuse/disorient the audience. Using shots from both sides of the line of action without neutral shots or line crossing movement will confuse your audience.

***Exercise**: Analyze footage from your favorite films and notice how the camera stays on one side of the action. Characters on the right side of the frame always stay on the right side for a particular scene unless they move during one of the shots and/or the camera moves across the line of action.*

Screen Direction

The 180° Rule maintains screen direction when followed properly. Moving subjects must move the same direction between shots within the same scene or you lose continuity. Here again the line of action is in the direction they are moving and you have to shoot all shots from one side. Stay on one side of the moving object and you will maintain continuity. Shooting a neutral shot or crossing the line during a shot allows you to change the screen direction in just about any direction you want.

In the following two shots the subject must be going the same direction in each shot as shown. If you moved the camera to the opposite side for the second shot it would appear as if they are going the wrong way...back in the other direction.

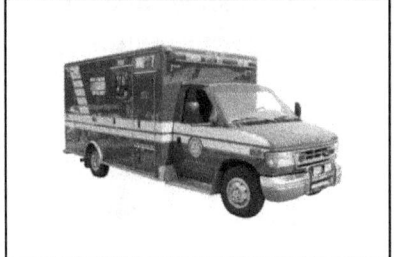
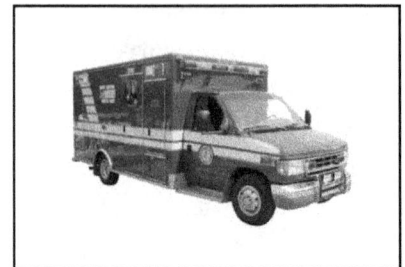

Ken Kiser

CHAPTER **23**

Lead Your Action

In shots with subject movement you want to leave part of the frame open in front of the subject in the direction the subject is moving. You are leading the action with the open portion of the frame. The camera must follow the movement and maintain this open area in the frame in the direction of the subject movement. Maintain the Rule of Thirds by framing the subject on the proper vertical line. If you were to leave more space behind the subject in the direction of movement then the framing would be off balance. It's very simple. Subject moving to the right: leave the right side of the frame open in front of the movement and position the subject on the left vertical frame. Subject moving to the left: leave the left side of the frame open in front of the movement and position the subject on the right vertical frame. Whichever direction the subject is moving leave that portion of the frame open and you will have continuity and a balanced frame. To end the shots, stop the camera movement and let the subject continue moving until exiting the frame or stop their movement while in the frame.

Anita Patterson Peppers   *Ken Kiser*

For a static camera shot with a static subject, the same method of leading your action should be applied. If the subject is looking to the right then the right side of the frame should be open.

Anita Patterson Peppers

Correct Positioning   Incorrect

The frame on the left is framed correctly. The frame on the right is not and the audience would expect someone/something to enter the frame from the left side and fill the open space behind the subject. This is often used in horror films to show that the killer is about to strike from behind the person.

Always maintain screen direction, especially when two subjects are talking to each other.

CHAPTER **24**

Overlap Your Action

When shooting action, it is best to shoot the action from different angles, giving you many options during editing. For example, a fight scene needs to look realistic and if you shoot only one shot it may actually have to be a real fight to look realistic. Shoot the fight from different angles and overlap the action from shot to shot. The last action from the first shot should be covered again by the second shot. If the action is of short duration then you can shoot the whole action again from different angles. Overlapping the action allows you to edit almost anywhere during the action, because you've covered it more than once. If you don't overlap the action you might be stuck with a shot you don't want and a shot that doesn't work. You could take the easy way out and use inserts or cut-aways to hide your problems, but you want to stay with the action if possible. Shoot the whole action if possible. You don't have the time or money to repeat every part of the action every time you shoot another shot. Something as simple as a kiss can be covered with additional angles. Shoot the kiss from different angles with different image sizes.

Shoot difficult action and dangerous stunts with more than one camera so you are able to capture the different angles. You may not have another chance to shoot some actions twice. If you're going to blow-up Grandma's house you'll only be able to blow up her house once, so get all your shots using multiple cameras.

CHAPTER **25**

Frame Entrances & Exits

When shooting shots where the subject will enter or exit the frame, start your camera before your subject enters the frame and stop it only after they have exited the frame. If your subject exits the frame in a shot and it is a MS, then they should enter the frame in the next shot in a MS. You want the subject size from one shot to the next to be similar if you are shooting similar camera angles for both shots.

The subject must enter the frame on the opposite side of the frame from which they exited in the preceding shot. Since the ambulance exits the right side of the frame in the first shot it must enter from the left side of the frame in the second shot.

 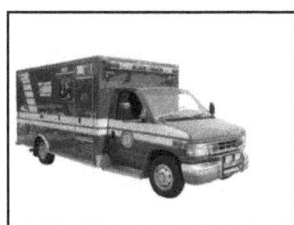

Ken Kiser

Exercise: *Analyze footage from your favorite films and make note of continuity shots. Notice the 180° Rule, screen direction, leading the action, overlapping the action, and frame entrances and exits. Find a subject to shoot footage with you. Set your camera on a tripod or use it handheld. Have them walk into frame then keep walking so you can practice leading the action by panning. Let them exit the frame. Start your next shots with the subject in the frame getting ready to move. You want to lead the action by starting your camera move just prior to the subject moving. You have to anticipate their movement.*

Shoot CU shots of two subjects in conversation: one subject in the frame at a time. Or use one subject and have them switch back and forth as if they are talking to their double. Have them wear a different wardrobe for the shots. Leave space in the front portion of the frame in the direction they are looking. Review and analyze your footage.

Shoot three angles of your subject getting in their car and make sure to overlap the action. Edit the shots together.

Light

Lighting is the most time consuming activity on a set. Lighting is used to create mood, texture, style, direct attention to a portion of the frame, etc. The director and cinematographer should have previously communicated/coordinated the look and lighting setup they are trying to achieve with each shot. If you are the director and cinematographer then you get to make all the decisions. By now you should realize the importance of pre-production. You have to know how you want your scenes lit, because any indecision will cost you hours each and every day.

First on the agenda is a note about **safety**. Lights are extremely hot and can be very dangerous to work with. If you've ever been on a set and experienced a **fire** then you know that most people will panic. You need to be ready. If a light catches on fire the first thing you must do is **unplug the light** or cut the power to the light. Then extinguish the fire using a fire extinguisher. Safety on the set is rule number one. Have fire extinguishers ready on the set. Always have several pairs of leather gloves handy that will allow you to handle the hot lights. Discuss it with the cast and crew beforehand so they are prepared. Keep all flammable material away from lights.

Painting with light is the phrase many cinematographers use to describe their passion. Writers use words. Cinematographers use light. You can manipulate the audience by manipulating the lighting to create the mood and atmosphere. Light each subject according to their personality. The wrong lighting on a subject can send the wrong message to the audience. Lighting will not be constant throughout your film. As a subject's personality changes so should their lighting. As your scenes change the lighting needs to change. Each shot may require a new lighting setup. Since your subplot/theme is the real story in your film, lighting should be focused on the subplot/theme. For example let's say you want to shoot a comedy with a dramatic subplot/theme so therefore, your lighting could be more dramatic. It might not be full-on dramatic lighting since your film is a comedy, but if you can light for your subplot/theme then you are impacting the audience with your lighting.

Light is energy. Have you ever been to Las Vegas? The experts in Vegas know that light keeps people awake! It's lit like daylight 24 hours per day. Walk out into the sun and it wakes you up. The audience feeds off of the light. If you want them to have energy...just add light. The audience will always look to the brightest area of your shots. Your Center of Interest should have the most light. Bright colors and bright lights always draw more attention. Know where you want the audience looking so you can emphasize those areas of the frame.

Lighting should not be noticed by the audience unless it is wrong. Light can be used as a character in a film as it was in the film *Insomnia*. Light played an integral part.

Exercise*: Study paintings as well as film for lighting. See how the artists use light to give contrast and how the light hits their subjects. Study the paintings in detail.*

CHAPTER **26**

Types of Lighting

Lighting is usually referred to as either hard or soft. In between hard and soft light is every combination that can be created. There are an infinite number of lighting fixtures that can be used to achieve your look. Low-budget shoots may not be able to afford professional lighting equipment, but you can build many of your own lights as well as use household lights and construction lights. Get creative.

Hard Lighting

Hard light goes directly from the light source to the subject without diffusing the light. Diffusing means to scatter, spread or filter. A simple example of hard light would be a bare light bulb. Hard light is usually a direct and small source of light. It is much grittier, tense, and more dramatic than soft light. Hard light casts hard, dark shadows. On a clear day the sun is a hard light source.

Soft Lighting

Hard light can be turned into soft light by ensuring it is not directly striking the subject. A bare light bulb covered by a lamp shade produces soft light because the shade diffuses the light. The sun on an overcast day becomes a softer light source because it is diffused by the cloud cover. Interior lights can be diffused using material, screens, scrims, filters, gels, etc. If you are working on a low budget you may not have access to all the lighting options you need when shooting, so learning how to soften light will be to your benefit. Placing diffusion in front of any light before it strikes the subject will soften it and decrease the harshness. The more diffusion in front of a light the softer the light gets. Light that is bounced off of a wall or a bounce board is also softened. A bounce board can simply be a white piece of art foam board or poster board held by hand or by other means. Be careful when bouncing light off of a colored wall or colored bounce board, because it will change the color of the light. Shadows cast by soft light are not as strong as hard light shadows. Soft light scatters to fill more area and is a much more natural looking light. If you want a softer more peaceful look then use soft light. Soft light is often used to make someone look younger, because it smoothes out wrinkles on a person's face and body.

__Exercise__: Buy a piece of foam board or poster board. Buy one white piece and one bright colored piece such as yellow or blue. Practice bouncing light onto objects from any source of light such as a lamp or overhead light. Notice how it softens once you bounce it. Place a piece of paper (wax paper or diffusion material) a short distance in front of the light (watch out for heat/fire) and notice how it diffuses the light. Place a piece of colored diffusion in front of the light and notice how it changes the color of the light.

CHAPTER **27**

Basic Lighting Setup

Setting up your lights can be a daunting task if you don't understand lighting basics. The traditional Basic Lighting Setup is a three light arrangement. This is where you want to start. The three lights making up the basic setup are the key light, fill light and back light. The following overhead shows the basic setup with key and fill lights on opposite sides of the camera and a back light highlighting the area behind the subject.

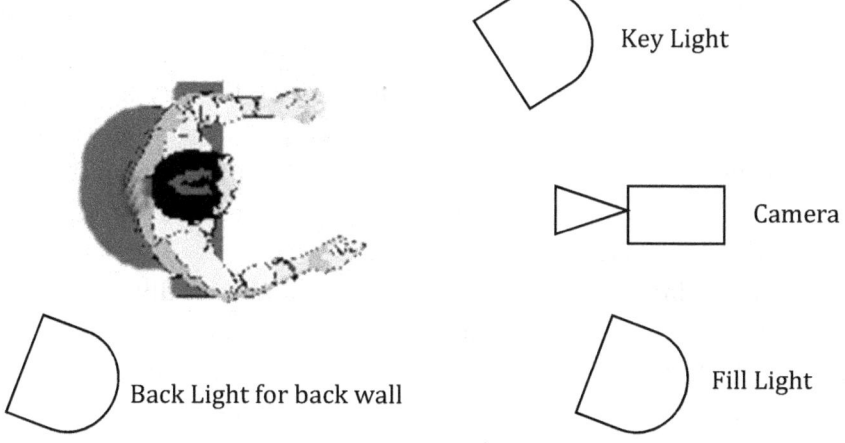

This pattern is repeated over a large set. If you need 3 key lights, common sense would tell you to use 3 fill lights and 3 backlights. That is not a bad assumption, but it really comes down to the purpose of each of these lights. The use of each light in combination with the others is the main point. You might have 2 key lights, 10 fill lights, and 2 back lights or 1 key light, 5 fill lights and 20 back lights on your setup. It all depends on the setup you want. What you need to understand is the **purpose** of each light. Feel free to break away from this traditional setup, but you need to learn it first.

Key Light

You want to start your lighting setup with placement of your key light(s) then add in additional lights as needed. The key light is the main (brightest/most intense) source of light in any shot and its purpose is to light the Main Character. The key light is usually hard and more direct light. When you're painting with light the f-stop of your key light would be the largest of any light used in a shot. Outdoors the sun would be your key light.

Fill Light

The fill light is positioned on the opposite side of the camera from the key light. It provides less light (smaller f-stop) than the key light and is used to fill in dark spots/shadows caused by the key light or other sources. The fill light is usually a softer light and covers more area. To avoid flat lighting it is common to have at least a two f-stop difference between your key light and fill light when measured on your Main Character's face. That is simply a standard.

You determine what style of lighting you want by the difference in light intensities between the key, fill and other lights. Remember the f-stops 1, 1.4, 2, 2.8, 4, 5.6, 8, 11, 16, 22. There are smaller and larger f-stop numbers, but this range is what you would normally see on your light meter. Of course you will see fractions along with the main numbers.

To better understand the f-stop difference assume your Main Character is standing between the key light and fill light and you want an f-stop

BASIC LIGHTING SETUP

difference of two f-stops. If you measure the side of their face that the key light illuminates and get an f-stop reading of 8, then you would want the reading on the fill light side of their face to be 4. If your key light measured 5.6 then you want your fill to measure 2.8. You may want more contrast and if that is the case use a three or more f-stop difference between key and fill. In that case if your key light f-stop reading is 8 then you would want a fill light f-stop reading of 2.8 or less. Understand?

Back Light

To add more depth and dimension to your shots use back lights. The back lights are usually placed above your set shining down on your subjects and shining on back walls in order to provide separation between your subjects and the walls. The back lights, as well as the fill lights, are also used to eliminate dark shadows, unless you want dark shadows. Back lights can be used to highlight the top surfaces of your subjects.

Other lights

Source Light

A light that is part of the scene as well as being a source of light for the scene. Examples are lamps, candles, streetlights, car headlights, a flashlight, fireplace, etc. It is a prop as well as a light source.

Set light

A light that is used to illuminate the walls and furniture on a set

Kicker Light

A type of back light used to add light wherever it is needed. You'll hear the phrase, "Put a kicker on it." It means to add some light to the area being discussed. They are placed on the opposite side of the key light and usually lower to the floor than back lights.

Obie Light/Ring Light

A small light mounted on top of the camera or even on the lens, used to put light into a subject's eyes. The eyes tell the story. A **Ring Light** is used for the same purpose as an Obie. It is a small ring with small bulbs around the circumference of the ring. Bulbs can be added/removed to the ring in order to provide the correct amount of light.

If you have a lot of subject movement and/or camera movement throughout a room move your lights as far away from the action as possible so they don't show up in your shots. You might have to use bounced/diffused light. Check exposures (f-stops) along the movement path to make sure you have proper light levels where you want them.

The following images show some of the best and most commonly used lighting equipment. The Chimera and Kino lights shown are soft lighting fixtures. The Arri light shown can be used as a flood or spot light...hard light or soft light by diffusing or bouncing.

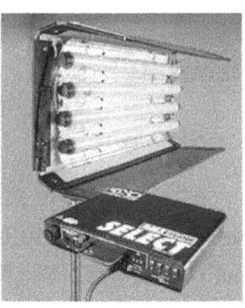

Chimera Lighting   *Arri Group*   *Kino Flo, Inc.*

CHAPTER **28**

Lighting Contrast

You have to determine how much contrast you want in each shot and in your film as a whole. Contrast is the difference between bright and dark areas in each shot. The areas of your frame that you don't light can be more important than the areas that you do light! The two types of lighting contrast are called high key and low key lighting.

High Key

High key lighting means a low contrast or small difference between light and dark areas in your shots including the way you light your subjects. Most of the shot is filled with light and there are few if any shadows. High key lighting is most often used for comedy, daytime shooting, TV sitcoms and anything bright and happy. Subjects' faces generally don't have much of an f-stop difference between both sides of their face. The face is not lit evenly (flat), but it doesn't have much contrast. The key and fill lights provide a similar amount of lighting, but the key light is always the dominant light.

Anita Patterson Peppers

Low Key

Low key lighting means a high contrast or big difference between light and dark areas in your shots. There would be a large difference between the amount of light provided by the key and fill lights. Once again the key light is the dominant light source in a shot. Most dramas use low-key lighting. Low key lighting provides a tense atmosphere, moody, evil, tragic, heavy shadows, night-time lighting. Faces are often lit bright on one side and dark on the other side to give a dramatic punch.

Anita Patterson Peppers   *Luis Tejo*

Flat

Lighting that is even across the frame. There are no shadows, no depth, no dimension, not creative looking light. Rarely would you want to use flat lighting in your film.

LIGHTING CONTRAST

Exercise*: Analyze several different genres of films...especially comedies versus dramas and notice the different lighting contrast for each film. Remember to turn off the sound! Do the filmmakers bring out the sub-plot/theme with their lighting? Watch older black and white films for lighting contrast.*

CHAPTER **29**

Lighting Placement

Where you place your lighting in regards to your subject determines the impact on your audience. You always start building your lighting setup with your main light source which is your key light. Then fill in the rest of the scene with fill and other lights, but none of these lights are as strong and bright as the key light. Consider the angle of the lighting just as you do for the angle of the camera and angle of the movement, etc. Consider how light falls on your subjects. Add dimension and depth by backlighting, side lighting and adding shadows. The shadows should look natural to the audience.

Where should you place your **key light?** Placing it in any of the following positions impacts your audience as explained.

Back Lighting

Placing your key light directly behind your subject and shining towards the camera outlines the subject. It gives a religious, angelic look, a kind of a halo effect, a silhouette. It can provide a romantic scene with softer light coming from behind your subjects. Using back lighting at night outlines the subject adding a mysterious figure in the dark night. Do not confuse back lighting with back lights. Back lighting refers to where you place your key light.

Clara Natoli   *Sanjay Pindiyath*

Frontal lighting

Placing your key light straight on in front of your subject makes your subject look flat, because the lighting has no contrast and it compresses or squeezes everything from front to back. This is not recommended for most shots.

Side Lighting

Placing your key light at the side of your subject adds depth, drama, texture, and dimension to your subject. It can cast heavy shadows if other lighting is not used to balance out some of the light.

Luis Tejo   *Anita Patterson Peppers*

Top Lighting

Placing your key light directly above your subject, such as the noon sun, produces deep dark shadows under your subject's chin, nose and in

LIGHTING PLACEMENT

the eye sockets. The noon sun is not the best time of day to shoot unless you want those shadows. You can eliminate the shadows by using bounce boards below your subject to reflect sunlight up onto their face.

Clara Natoli *Anita Patterson Peppers*

Under Lighting

Placing your key light underneath your subject causes the subject to look evil. Remember your camping trips and Halloween...someone would always place a flashlight under their chin and scare everyone.

__Exercise__: Study light. Turn on a light and study how it falls on objects around it, etc. Place an object under the light, then next to the light and then above the light to see how placement changes the look. Notice how the sunlight comes through windows in your residence. Notice how it flows into the room and strikes the walls, floor and objects in the room. Change the curtains/blinds and notice what happens to the light. Analyze films and see if you can determine how they lit a particular scene. Where did they place their key light? You can tell because it provides the most light in any shot. Did they place it behind the subject? In front? To the side? Above or below? Find a black and white film and study the light. Black and white films make it much easier to see the light and how the lighting is used to enhance the shots. Pause/freeze-frame your footage if you need to in order to study the lighting.

Once you know where to place your main source of light (key light) then and only then can you build your lighting design.

CHAPTER **30**

Lighting Choices

Your lighting decisions for each shot depend on the impacts you want to have on your audience. Determine what you want by answering the following questions for each shot and scene.
- What do you want normally exposed?
- What do you want overexposed? Bright areas draw more audience attention.
- What do you want underexposed? Dark areas draw less audience attention.
- Do you want shadows? Where? What kind...dark, light?
- What mood do you want? Is this a drama, comedy, thriller, etc.?
- What is your subplot/theme? Do you want to light for subplot/theme?
- Do you want hard light, soft light, high key, low key, etc.?

Now you know how you can impact the audience simply by using light. For example, a subject's light should change throughout the film depending on their emotional state. If a subject starts out happy, upbeat, energetic, then their eyes would be fully lit as well as their face, etc. If their life starts to take a turn for the worse then you would start to remove light. If they hit rock bottom then they would have little if any light in their eyes, shadows and little if any light on their face. Lighting faces are most important, especially the eyes. Darker hair/skin requires more light for detail. You can impact the audience with your lighting without using one word of dialog.

Within any given scene you want to try and shoot all shots for that scene at the same f-stop and the same lighting setup. Otherwise you may have continuity problems, because lighting won't match up when you try to edit shots together.

Most cinematographers like to shoot in the 2.8 to 5.6 f-stop range to achieve the best look for their shots and because most lenses perform best within this range of settings. Remember this f-stop range when lighting your shots.

__Exercise:__ Go through your script and write down the emotions you want in each scene. Take notes for the type of lighting that will help you achieve those emotions.

CHAPTER 31

Power Requirements

Unless you can afford to use generators you will have to determine how many lights your location's electrical system can handle without popping circuit breakers or blowing fuses. Circuit breakers and fuses are used to prevent overloading of electrical circuits. The breaker will pop or the fuse will blow in order to prevent a short circuit (fire hazard). It's like pulling on a piece of string. Sooner or later if you pull hard enough the string will break. The same thing happens when you overload an electrical circuit. Too much load and it will pop the breaker or blow the fuse. Breakers can be reset, but fuses have to be replaced. Know your locations and whether they have circuit breakers or fuses and where the breaker panel/fuse box is located. Be prepared to reset breakers or replace fuses if you use the power from the location.

First you should determine which wall outlets are powered by which circuits. You can do this by simply plugging a lamp into the electrical outlets in each room and then throwing/moving the breaker to the open/off position or removing the fuses one by one. Your light will go off when you have the right circuit. Check every outlet and make sure you label it with its appropriate circuit. Once you have matched outlets and circuits you can look at the breaker/fuse and determine the amperage rating. It should list the amperage directly on it. Most common for homes in the US are 15 to 30 amps per circuit. This is the amperage each circuit can handle for all of the outlets combined on that circuit. If you plug in too many lights on one circuit then you will pop the breaker or blow the fuse.

The below formula will help you determine the amount of load each circuit can handle. Check your power standards for the region of the world in which you live. This formula is only for areas using 110 Volt circuits.

How much power is available for your lights on each circuit?

Formula

Watts = Volts x Amps

If you know the amp rating of each breaker/fuse then all you have to do is multiply that rating times the voltage. Since the US standard voltage is 110 volts you multiply the amp rating times 110 to determine how many watts each circuit can handle. It is best to use 100 as the voltage, because this gives you some margin of safety. Some breakers/fuses may trip/blow at or below their rating depending on their age and sensitivity.

Example: You have a circuit with a 15 amp breaker/fuse. If you multiply 100 volts x 15 amps you get 1500 watts. You can plug a total of 1500 watts of lighting into the outlets for that one circuit. That means you can plug in three 500 watt lights; or one 1000 watt light and one 500 watt light; or fifteen 100 watt lights. Determine the watts for each light and then you can determine where to plug them in if you know how much wattage each circuit can handle.

Exercise*: Find the breaker box/fuse box in your residence and determine the size of the breakers/fuses. Then determine how much lighting capacity you have for each circuit. How many watts can each circuit handle? Now that you know the circuit capacity, get your hands on some lights and experiment. If you do not have access to professional lights buy some construction lights. Use lamps in your home. Find clamp-on lights and make your own stands out of wood or PVC piping if necessary. The main factor is to experiment and get creative. Practice using lights in combination and see what you can do. Place diffusion in front of the lights in order to diffuse/filter the lights.*

CHAPTER **32**

Colors of Light

Whether you knew it or not different lights (bulbs, fixtures, elements) put out different colors of light. Light color is measured in degrees Kelvin (temperature). For example, sunlight is measured at 5400 K°. Your naked eye does not see the different colors of light like your recording media. It will react differently to the different colors of light. What looks normal to you may come out blue, yellow, orange, green, etc. Non-film cameras allow you to white balance the camera to match the color of the light you are using. Film is not as easy to use, because you can't white balance the camera by simply pushing a button. Film stocks are rated to match a certain color of light. If you use different colors of light then you have to use colored filters on the camera, or gels on the lights, in order to match the light color to your film.

Exterior Lighting

The color of the sun changes throughout the course of a day. The sun in the early morning shows up more yellow than the sun at noon (blue) and the sun in late afternoon (orange/red). If you shoot different shots at different times of the day they may not match up due to the color changes of the sun. Check the natural light at your locations at different times of the day and shoot test shots at the time of day you think you will be shooting. If you need to come back and do re-shoots then you should shoot at the same time of the day and year, because of the color changes.

Exercise: Look at the sunlight in the morning, at noon and late in the day. Can you see the difference in color? Shoot several minutes of exterior footage at sunrise, noon, and sunset. Then review all of your footage and notice the difference in colors. You must know how your recording media reacts to the different exterior colors of the sun depending on the time of day. The colors will also vary depending on the time of year you shoot. It's important to keep good records of the time of day and the dates you shoot in order to match your shots.

Interior Lighting

You can control your lighting if, and only if, you eliminate any exterior light entering the set. If you mix and match different types of lighting elements, fixtures, bulbs, etc., then you can expect color variations in your shots. For example fluorescent lights put out a green tint. If you look close enough you can see it. Mixing a fluorescent light with a soft white bulb will give off a different color of light than if you only used one or the other. If you are using large professional lighting fixtures make sure you know the color temperature of each light fixture and the number of hours on each element/bulb. Some elements/bulbs degrade as they age, thus changing the light color, so be careful when using older light elements/bulbs. If you mix different light sources across a scene you could get a color change as you move through a scene. Some filmmakers want to decrease their light by using a simple dimmer switch, but that can cause the light to change color. Be careful when using a simple commercial dimmer. It's best to use professional dimmer equipment.

Exercise: Shoot several minutes of footage using fluorescents, several minutes using soft light bulbs and then regular light bulbs. Once again, do not change any camera settings such as the white balance. Analyze your footage for the color differences in your shots.

Sound

Film is a visual medium, but ever since the evolution of talking pictures the audience expects great sound in their films. Dialog, music and sound effects allow you to manipulate your audience almost as easily as you can with your images. Create and plan your audio just as you would your visuals. Your audience will thank you.

CHAPTER **33**

Sound

Location sound recording is often overlooked by many filmmakers because everyone seems to focus their attention on the cinematography. Sound recording is as important, if not more important, than the cinematography. Bad sound is not easy to correct. You can loop the dialog, but it can be tough to match the location dialog without the equipment, time and budget to handle it. Even then it is difficult. Always check to make sure your sound is being recorded properly.

Sound Mixer

The mixer is the person responsible for sound recording. There are two ways of recording sound. If you are shooting on film then you will be recording the sound on a separate recorder. Then the sound is synced with the picture (image) for editing. If you are shooting on a digital camera, you can most likely record sound along with the picture. A separate sound recorder may be used as well. One problem with recording sound into your camera is if the mic cable is attached to the camera. If you are trying to do handheld camera moves, rehearse your camera moves with your mic and cable. If you have trouble accomplishing camera moves with the mic attached you may have to use wireless mics, a separate sound recorder or shoot some shots MOS. It's best to use a camera that allows XLR connectors for connecting your sound cables.

XLR connectors provide for a virtually noise-free audio signal so no humming noises or unwanted sounds interfering with the signal.

Sound Mixing

Entails using a mixing board (mixer) in between the mic and the recording device. The mixer allows adjustments of the audio signal during recording. Is a mixer necessary? No! Often times an inexperienced mixer can ruin the sound so keep that in mind. Then you end up trying to fix it in post-production if it's possible. People have ruined dialog for entire films by mixing. You can get by without using a mixer during shooting. Some people swear by them, but some people like to have equipment, whether it is needed or not.

Boom Operator

Handles the mic, placing it in the proper location for recording the dialog. The mic is mounted in a pistol grip or other shock mount fixture and then the mount is attached to a boom pole. The shock mount prevents vibration from inducing noise into the mic. Boom poles can be made or bought depending on your budget. A cheap boom pole can be made from an extendable paint pole.

The best mic to use is a shotgun mic. They are very directional, meaning they record sound in one direction or small area: the direction/area in which you are pointing the mic. They limit background noise coming from other directions. It is a multi-purpose mic that can be used for all dialog and any sounds you need to capture. Large shotgun mics can be used when shooting in extremely noisy environments such as train stations, airports, etc. You can use one short shotgun mic for your entire shoot. Use a mic windscreen during exterior shooting to prevent wind or even the slightest breeze from inducing noise into your mic. Following are images of a shotgun mic, mic windscreen and mic shock mount.

Sennheiser mic   Rycote mic support

Lavaliere mics and wireless mics can be used where a shotgun mic cannot. They are small and can be hidden almost anywhere, especially on your subjects. Lavaliere mics require a mic cable, whereas wireless mics don't. Choose the best equipment you can afford so you can record the best possible sound.

Sound Recording Tips

- Try and place the mic within 3 feet of your subject during dialog shots. Place it above them with the mic aimed down at their mouth. Do not place the mic level with their mouth or you will pick up unwanted popping sounds such as lips smacking or mouth opening noises. If you cannot place the mic above the subject then place it below them aimed up at their mouth.
- Make sure your camera operator knows where the mic is located so the mic doesn't show up in any shots. Do a visual check before each shot to properly position your mic to ensure it is out of frame. There is no excuse for this happening on a low-budget film, let alone a Hollywood blockbuster.
- Place sound blankets (thick, absorbing material) or any kind of blankets on bare floors to prevent echo and unwanted noise. Place blankets on walls if you need to cut down on sound bouncing off the walls and into the direction of the mic.
- Avoid pointing the mic too close to a wall, because of the echo from dialog/noise bouncing off the wall back into the mic. Point the mic down and away from the wall.

- When recording in exterior locations do not point the mic towards busy streets or else you may pick up unwanted traffic noise.
- Avoid pointing the mic at the camera, because it may pick up the sound of the running camera, depending on the camera's noise level. You can blimp the camera if required to eliminate camera noise. Blimping means sound proofing. You can use a blanket, coat or thick material to deaden the sound.
- When shooting indoors, unplug any appliances that may add noise to the room. Refrigerators, heaters, phones, air conditioners, etc., have ruined many shots. After each shot, plug them back in, but during shooting you must silence them. Quiet all cell phones.
- Allow for a minimum of 8 seconds of sound pre-roll before beginning the actual scene being shot. This means to start your camera/sound recorder and let it run for a minimum of 8 seconds before starting the actual scene.
- Announce each shot so it is recorded on the sound media.
- At the beginning of a new sound roll announce the roll number, the film title and the date. The term roll means any format of recording media you are using.
- It is best to record sound effects on separate recordings instead of during dialog, so that you don't interrupt or ruin your dialog shots. If you need a gunshot then record an actual gunshot or buy the sound effects you need. There are many outlets for buying sound effects. Search the internet.

For each location make sure you record **wild sound**. Wild sound is simply done by turning on the sound recording equipment and recording the sound (room tone) of the room/location, without anyone making any noise. Total silence for at least one minute if not two. This way you have that specific room tone for each location for use during editing. If you go to each location you can easily hear the tone of that location, especially locations with background traffic noise. If you need to re-record dialog or replace sound for certain shots then this wild sound will give you the needed background tone. This will allow you to match sound for all shots.

Sound effects (foley) are added during the editing phase. Foley is covered in the Editing Chapter.

Music

Do not play/record music during dialog shots. Add the music during editing so you don't ruin the dialog.

Post

You've reached a huge milestone in your filmmaking...post-production. The chaos known as production has ended and you are settling in for your edit. Even though the hectic pace of production is in your rearview mirror, believe it or not you will probably miss it. You will miss the action. You will miss the people in your cast and crew. It can be a lonely time sitting in an editing bay or in your residence by yourself or with an editor building your film. Know that this is not going to be your only film and that you will be back in production on another as soon as you can. Settle in and get ready to push for the summit...the final cut!

CHAPTER **34**

Editing

The simplistic definition of editing is joining two shots together. Two shots together develop a meaning, an emotion, an idea. Editing a film involves putting a series of shots together then shaping, tightening, building scenes and sequences, inter-cutting parallel actions and images, developing pacing and rhythm. Edits should communicate different viewpoints and thoughts, build drama, conflict, tension, comedy and energy, and show a flow of time and changes of place, etc.

Editing depends on everything you do prior to editing. You write a script to shoot and you shoot a script to edit. So essentially you write to edit. Editing is very much like writing, because writing requires re-writing and editing requires re-editing. Great editing requires you to rework a piece and not lose interest in it as you view it over and over and over. Editing takes all of your shots and builds your film. Editing brings your film to life. You are Dr. Frankenstein. You have all of these parts (shots) and you have to combine them to create life. Hopefully you get the parts you need during production to make a great film, instead of a monster. Your pre-production and production are designed to allow your editing to go as smoothly as possible. If you have captured the required footage that tells the story of your script then you should not have to go back into production mode and re-shoot. You are now set to build your masterpiece. It's like building a house. You have everything you need at the construction site. No more running back to the lumber yard for more and more. All the pieces are ready to be assembled. Editing should be transparent to the audience just as your camerawork should be transparent.

Where you place each shot in the film has to be thought out. You can't randomly place your shots. Where you place them determines the reaction and the meaning the audience will derive from your film. Experiment with your shot placement. The shots by themselves have little meaning. To better understand the principles of editing let's go back to the 1920's and two Russian filmmakers named Lev Kuleshov and Vsevolod Pudovkin. They determined that the placement of shots determines how the audience reacts. They took four different shots and edited them together two shots at a time, and developed three different meanings. The shots were: a man's face with little if any expression, a girl playing, a woman in a coffin, and a bowl of soup. They edited the shot of the bowl of soup to the shot of the man's face and the meaning derived was his hunger. They edited the shot of the coffin to the shot of the man's face and he was in mourning. They edited the shot of the girl playing to the shot of the man's face and he was a joyful parent. All of these meanings were derived from the same shot of an expressionless face. You derive meaning from where you place your shots. The meaning is open to interpretation by the audience, but your goal is to impact the majority of them in the same way.

Tell the best story you can. You have to know if things make sense for your audience. Can you grab your audience and keep them interested? Can you keep them guessing about what is coming next? If you edit several shots together the audience will be expecting a certain payoff. Find ways to delay that payoff to keep them in suspense and keep them thinking. If everything is resolved quickly in the next scene following the expectation, then they will get bored. The expectations for an audience are like the expectations of a child on their birthday. If a child wants a new bike for their birthday their expectations are high that they will receive a bike. You give them present after present, but no bike. The child is anticipating it but you have kept them guessing. Finally, when you give them the bike they are ecstatic. The build up to the bike was incredible.

They were on the edge of their seat thinking they weren't going to get their bike. Just when they thought all was lost...boom...out came the bike. They reached the end of the story...they got their bike...the party is over. If you had given them the bike first they would have rode off on it without the anticipation...without the rest of the party...without the rest of the presents...without the journey. You have to determine how long to delay the prize. Your audience walks into the theater expecting certain things. Don't automatically give them what they want. Make them earn it. Keep them guessing! Take the audience on a rollercoaster ride that they will never forget.

Learn to Edit

The simplest way to learn editing is to analyze films with the sound off, which is what you have been doing throughout this whole book. You have been training your brain to edit from page one.

To learn to be an editor you have to edit. Just like being a car salesman. If you want to be a car salesman then you have to get out there and sell cars. You can sit in a classroom for ten years, but until you get out there and do it you won't learn much! Shoot footage and edit! There are no editing rules etched in stone. Editing is based on experimenting with your material. It takes trial and error. Most of your knowledge will come from your own experience and from your ability to get the emotions out of the footage you have. Go with your instincts. An infinite amount of possibilities exist in your footage and you must choose the best images and sounds to use for the final cut of your film. You have to develop a bond with your footage. Yes, you and your footage will become the best of friends. There will be times when things go right and times when they don't. You must know what you want your scenes, sequences and film to do. What are you trying to say? What message are you telling the audience? Why did you end the shot when you did and start the next shot when you did? How will you transition from one shot to the next? Which shots do you lengthen by adding additional shots and which shots do you shorten? Where should you place each shot? What is the pacing of your film? What is the rhythm of your film? What kind of sound effects and music will you add? You have in mind what you want and you edit one shot to another shot and determine if it measures up to what you expected. Editing can take longer than any other portion in the making of a film, and rightly so. It takes patience, persistence, and focus. It is a tedious but exciting experience to see your footage and build it into your film. Production mode is always chaos: running on empty, no time to think, always trying to catch up. Editing takes you back to thinking mode. Take your time. Don't get in a hurry just to make a film festival date. Don't rush and put a bad product out into the world. You want your film to be great, and editing is where you make your film greater than you expected.

Review Your Footage

The first step to take is to review all of your footage. During your initial review of each shot try to find the moment...the emotion...the climax in each shot. Analyze every take and determine the best takes. Doing this will help you eliminate some of your footage before you start to edit, but you will still have problems deciding which takes to keep and which takes to set aside. Some decisions are easy and some decisions will cost you plenty of sleep. Eventually you have to make your final choices about which shots to keep in the film.

Once you have gone through your footage then you start to assemble your film or **cut** as it's called. The first time you watch an edited piece take note of the emotional impact it has on you. Write down your thoughts, because once you've seen that edited footage 100 times it may lose its impact. You can get so involved in your footage you lose all feeling for it and the only way to remember those first feelings is to write them down. Otherwise you may start second guessing your earlier decisions.

Your job is to edit two shots together to develop a meaning for the audience and have them believing your film is one continuous story. The audience has to be able to fill in the gaps between any two shots in your edit. If the audience is able to fill in the gaps you have succeeded. For example, you see a character in New York packing their luggage and the next shot they are arriving in Los Angeles...most people can fill in that time (hours, days) and space gap (3000 miles) and understand they flew, drove or rode a train to LA. You don't have time to show the whole trip. You are compressing time and space. Some people might not be able to connect the dots...fill the gap...make sense from one shot to the next. Some get it and some don't. Unfortunately most films today don't offer up much of a thinking challenge for the audience. Challenge them! Let them think.

When and How to Cut

You have to have a reason to make a cut: emphasizing something, adding meaning, drama, comedy, mystery, suspense, info, intensity, etc. Once you find that reason then cut and move on to the next shot. The main action must be strengthened by cutting. If you aren't bringing more attention to someone/something then why cut? What are you adding when you cut? Be careful when cutting dialog, because you may be ruining the whole message of that dialog or its connection with another part of the story.

Find a good beginning and ending for each cut. You have to determine how you want to transition from one shot to the next and make it appear continuous. Transitions can involve images, audio or both. There are different types of transitions you can use, but cuts and dissolves are used the most.

Transitions

Emotions

They are number one. Find the emotions in your footage and when you do it's time to edit/cut. Show the audience those emotions, then move on.

The Look

A common time to cut is to cut on the look of a character. Everyone has been given a look by someone...a look that said it all. You knew exactly what they were thinking...good or bad. Hold the shot as long as the character is thinking that same thought. Watch their eyes. The eyes always tell the truth. The eyes will tell you what they are thinking and when they change thoughts.

Shot Matching/Shot Contrast

Putting matching shots together gives a smooth and more eye-pleasing edit. Matching shots means cutting from one size image to a similar sized image (MS to MS), or cutting from one image to a related image in relation to subject matter, color, lighting, etc. Putting contrasting shots together gives a dramatic edit...such as cutting from a small image (LS) to a large image (CU) or cutting from a dark shot to a bright shot.

Continuity Editing/Cutting

Simply means matching cuts to make the action appear to have a continuous flow. The film flows smoothly across the screen and is easy to follow.

Action Cutting

You must match the action when cutting so the action appears to have a continuous flow. If you are going to cut, always cut just as a portion of the action is starting. For example, if you want to edit two shots (LS & MS) of a person running, the cut must make it appear as though the running action is seamless. Starting with the LS...you decide to cut when the right arm of the subject is coming forward. The MS must start a fraction after the right arm starts coming forward. Otherwise it will look like a piece of the action is missing if you start too late (jump cut) or it will look like part of the action is being repeated if you start too early (double action).

Rhythm

Shot rhythm is determined by shot duration, frequency and movement (camera & subject) much like the beats in music. Listen to music...not the words, but the music. Notice how the rhythm repeats itself, but yet it also changes throughout a song. A film is the same way.

Pacing

Fast pacing doesn't mean a lot of quick cuts. A shot can be fast paced by the action in the shot or the emotions in the shot without having any cuts. A slow paced scene may involve many cuts.

Cuts

Straight cutting from one shot to the next. Simply butting two shots up against each other. One shot ends and the next one begins. The most basic of all edits.

Dissolves

Two shots (may include sound) which are overlapped so one shot fades out of view as the other shot comes into view. For a short period of time the audience can see both shots overlapping each other. Dissolves provide for a smoother transition than cuts, because of the gradual change from one shot to the next shot instead of an abrupt change. They can be used for a short passage of time or a location change.

Inserts

A shot usually related to the main action (Cut-Ins) is inserted after another shot. Cut-Aways are shots that also can be inserted, but they do not relate to the main action of the shot/scene. Most of the time an insert shows the audience exactly what the subject is looking at or thinking about. It's a shot the audience is expecting to see. The subject reacts to something and then, you show the audience what the subject is reacting too.

Wipes

It's like wiping off a table with a cloth. One shot wipes across the screen and pushes the other shot out of the frame. The wipe may come from any side of the frame.

Fades

Fades are usually used to start a film (Fade In from black) and to end it (Fade Out to black), but can be used anywhere. They separate one shot from the next shot by showing a passage of time and place. Usually the fade is to a black screen/frame then back to another shot. A fade can be used to edit/cover up two shots that don't have a good way of being edited and have no relation to each other. Fades slow down the momentum of the film. Be careful when using them to cover up the fact that your shots won't transition together.

Montage

A group of related, short shots used to show a long passage of time such as a child becoming an adult, a change of seasons, someone learning a skill to become an expert, an army training for battle, Rocky Balboa working out getting ready for the championship fight, etc.

Jump Cuts

Shots edited together with a horizontal angle change that doesn't follow the 30º Rule! There is no continuity from one shot to the next, because it is almost the same shot, but with a slightly different image size. Jump cuts provide a leap-frog effect towards a subject. Jump cuts are much more acceptable in today's fast-paced style of editing.

Audio/Sounds

Tie shots together using narration, dialog, sounds, speeches and music so sound flows across scenes.

Symbolic Images/Patterns

Group these together or spread them throughout your film to build a meaning or response from your audience. The film *Witness* used grain throughout the film to represent the peaceful and natural lifestyle of the Amish people. These symbols/patterns are a great way to represent your subplot/theme. Use them as little reminders to the audience of what your film is truly about.

Cross Cutting (Parallel Editing)

Two or more separate events/actions happening in separate places simultaneously or made to look like they are happening simultaneously. The shots go back and forth showing the two actions or two comparisons. Inter-cutting the two actions shows the progress of each action toward a final resolution/climax. For example, a person is sleeping and a burglar is creeping outside of the building, scenes of a raging fire and fire trucks racing to get there, two armies coming to battle. Horror movies show the killer stalking and the teenagers (soon-to-be victims) partying in the cabin. You can make comparisons, such as showing the contrast of Beverly Hills and Skid Row or an older person remembering younger days. Cross cutting is used to build tension, excitement, emotion, etc. As you get closer to the resolution/climax of the battle, or the two events meeting up, you want to make the cuts quicker and quicker. Editing directly from a LS to a CU as the climax approaches, will increase the impact, tension and pacing for the audience.

Expectations

Give the audience something to expect and then either give them what they expected or hold off from giving it to them in order to build tension, drama and anticipation. Eventually you have to give them what they expect or you will disappoint them. You have to resolve the expectation in some manner. You can't set them up and then not deliver. If a subject talks about something or looks at something then the audience is expecting to see it. Give it to them.

Editing Moving & Static Shots

Sometimes it can be tough to edit static and moving shots together, because it can be an abrupt change. This can be used for great impact on the audience also. Experiment with your shots to determine what you can and can't do. There are no exact rules for editing moving and static shots.

Sound Editing

Automated/Automatic Dialogue Replacement (ADR)

ADR is part of the editing process where new dialog is added into shots to replace bad dialog. The actors have to match their lips (lip sync) when recording the new replacement dialog. You can cut to reaction shots (coverage shots) for portions of the scene so you don't have to lip sync the entire dialog. See how important it is to shoot coverage? Wild sound is then added to give the shots the same location background tone.

Foley

Foley can make the difference between an amateurish sounding film and a professional sounding film. Foley includes sounds such as footsteps, doors closing, traffic noise, gunshots, screams and overall background noise of any sort. Use anything at your disposal to make the sounds for each scene. Walk across the type of surface you need with the mic down at your feet. Record the opening and closing of your car door. Creating foley can be a lot of fun and requires a bit of imagination.

Music

What type of music do you want for your film? What do you want your music to add to your film? If you are planning on using copyrighted songs then you will have to plan for it in your budget. Music rights can be incredibly expensive and most filmmakers will not be able to afford to use them. Do not use any music or lyrics from a song without prior approval. Contact the record companies to inquire about use and associated costs and to find out if they have any up-and-coming artists they are trying to promote. Tell them you are an up-and-coming filmmaker wanting to license their new artists. It is better to find musicians or new bands looking to get their music out into the mainstream. Films are a good source of marketing for them. Ask them to use their music for free or deferred payment. Have them sign a release, but allow them to retain all music rights. There are many talented unknowns waiting to be discovered. Find unrepresented bands, songwriters, singers, composers and musicians and work out a deal to use their music. You can also buy stock music for use in your film, but original music is always the better choice.

Building Sound Tracks

Build layers (tracks) of foley, music, dialog, etc., into your edit. Your edit will not resemble a finished film until you have added in the additional layers of sound.

Make sure you have other people view your edits and give you comments. Working on your film can consume you to the point that you cannot be objective about your film. You have been living inside the belly of the beast and need an objective opinion to help you see what you cannot see. You need additional sets of eyes to provide you with feedback.

Exercise: *Analyze footage of your favorite films and make note of the transitions from one shot to the next. When and how do they edit from shot to shot? What type of transitions are they using and do they involve pictures and sound? What does each edit tell you? Why do you think they cut one shot when they did and started the next shot when they did? What message do you get from each edit? Find where you wish the scene/shot would have been longer or cut sooner. How long are their shots? Can you feel, see and hear the rhythm/pacing?*

The first cut of your film is called a rough cut, because that's exactly what it is: a rough cut of your film. It may be three times as long as what you want in your final cut, but it's best to make your shots longer than necessary on your rough cuts and then scale them back. Some people like to work in sections, such as the first 10 minutes and keep revising it until it is complete. Others like to piece together all of their footage and then sit down and watch the whole rough cut of their film. You have to decide how you want to work. Trying to perfect one small section of your film prior to moving forward can often times stop your momentum from finishing your rough cut. It can be very similar to writing a rough draft of your script versus only writing and perfecting your first act. Most filmmakers finish a rough cut to give them the feeling of some accomplishment. Remember to reward yourself along the way and then get back to work. You will spend many days, months, maybe even years revising your edit until you get to your final cut.

Don't wait until you've finished your film to engage the business side of the industry. Be responsible for your film's success from beginning to end. Build up the anticipation with agents, managers, producers, studios, distributors, press and your audience. Begin marketing to them when you begin development of your script.

Your Finished Film

You went and did it...you finished your film! Congratulations. Everyone is patting you on the back and wanting to know when they can see it...when will it premiere...when will it be out for the world to see. Everyone wants to walk the red carpet with you and stay in your Malibu Beach house or Beverly Hills mansion. Wait just a minute! By finishing your film you've finished half the race. Now it's time to get into business mode so put on your business hat and finish the journey.

CHAPTER **35**

The Business Side

There's a reason it's called Show Business. It's all about business. You are dealing with people and businesses that have to make money. If they don't make money then they won't be in Show Business very long. The streets of the film industry are littered with failures. The business side of filmmaking is just as important as the creative side of filmmaking. Unfortunately, most filmmakers don't even give it a second thought until after they've finished their film. You need to be working on your marketing plan at the same time you are working on your shooting plan.

Marketing Plan

Developing an aggressive marketing plan for the business side of your film must include as many marketing avenues as you can possibly find: internet (film sites, your site, blogs, social networks), magazines, newsletters, posters, postcards, business cards, flyers, t-shirts, newspapers, interviews (radio, TV, magazines, newspapers, internet), parties (throw one), festivals, screenings, etc. The key to great marketing is knowing your targets. Who are the main targets for your film? If you don't know your targets then you will not succeed. Are you targeting your audience, agents, managers, studios, cable, producer reps/sales agents, distributors, entertainment lawyers...who? Create a huge awareness for your film. Network and schmooze.

You should be contacting every connection you can find during pre-production, production and post-production. Let them know where you are in your plan. Let them know you are taking action and proceeding forward. Don't waste their time. You're not asking for anything other than to notify them of your progress. Send them updates every 15 to 30 days detailing your progress so they keep your name in their memory. That way, once you finish your film, they will be more willing to look at your film prior to submittal to any festivals, markets or distributors. Keep your audience up to date so that they will be ready to see your film whenever and however it is released.

Most agencies and studios have independent film divisions whose job is to represent/buy independent films or help get them made. If you can make your own films they love you, because the effort for them is minimal. They like people with initiative. They like people who take action. Act like a professional and keep a positive attitude. If they won't acknowledge your existence then don't worry about it. Someone else will. Keep making films and moving forward.

Press

Press depends on you unless you can afford a publicist, but no one has the passion for your film as much as you do. You have to be a one-person press monster. Press covers many different avenues. Make sure you take still pictures throughout your shoot showing cast, crew and sets in order to be ready for press kits to be developed. Any still photos you provide to the press should include captions describing each photo. Have both black & white and color photos. Keep a journal of your experiences during your shoot. Contact every newspaper, magazine, newsletter and website related to the industry and make yourself available for an interview via phone, email or in person. Put together two types of press kits: an Electronic Press Kit (EPK) and a Written press Kit (WPK).

EPK

Includes: recorded interviews with cast, crew, director, etc. Make sure you shoot footage during shooting or set up a mock shooting to use as if it were the real thing. Remember this is storytelling. Press is also storytelling.

WPK

Includes: bios of everyone involved, a credits list of cast and crew, a synopsis (summary) of the film and written interviews of key cast and crew members, along with the director.

Distributors

Deal with the best of the best. Find other films similar to yours and determine who their distributor was and only deal with them. If you get an offer to sell your film try and get money up front: advanced sales money. If your distributor is serious about your film then they will give you money up front. Although it is getting tougher and tougher to get advanced sales money, you have to decide whether you want to sell your film to a distributor that will not give any. They may have other films to market but they must be serious about selling your film as well. In your contract/deal you want to get profit participation in box office, TV, cable, satellite, DVD, Video On Demand (VOD), educational markets, etc. You don't want to be responsible for the cost of audio masters, posters, advertising, prints, etc. Make sure the distributor is responsible for those costs. Make sure those costs are not deducted from your portion of the profits and put a limit on the other expenses you will have subtracted from your end. Your contract must have performance parameters in it that allow you to retain ownership rights to your film if they do not perform within a certain time limit as stated in the contract. Once that time limit has passed, without any progress on their part, you retain the rights to your film. That is only fair if they are not marketing your film.

What is your distributor's marketing plan for foreign and domestic distribution? Who will they be targeting? What markets? What kind of prediction do they have for your film as far as box office, sales, etc.? Do they want domestic and foreign rights? What other sales avenues does the contract cover? You should be very involved in their plan.

You might not want to give an exclusive all-rights deal to one distributor. Break up the domestic and foreign rights with different parties. Don't sign an exclusive deal for digital rights. You want to be able to sell on your own as well. This helps prevent one entity from controlling all-rights, especially if they are not performing to your expectations. There is no one-way to ensure the most success for your film. What may work for one film may not work for another.

The contract should cover the following line items.

Contract Line Items:

- Upfront Money
- Percent of the Box Office, TV & Cable, DVD, VOD, Rentals, Downloads, etc.
- Limit on Your Expenses and Deductions From Profits
- Domestic and Foreign Rights
- Contract Termination Date
- Rights to Your Film
- Audit rights so you can verify their records against what you were to receive

Get everything in writing. If anyone ever utters the words "trust me," do not trust them. What someone says and what someone does are usually two different things. If it's not in writing, it doesn't exist.

Self-distribution

Self distribution can a tough road to travel but it has been accomplished in the past and will continue to be done in the future, especially with new avenues for distribution. The future looks brighter every day for the independent filmmaker to retain ownership and self distribute. It requires you to deal with theaters, TV and cable networks, websites, advertising, etc. Sell your film from your own website. Use a fulfillment company for sales if you don't have the time or don't want to mail DVD's to the world. Fulfillment companies will do everything from marketing and sales to distribution.

Film Festivals

Festivals have been, and still are, great places to catch the eye of Hollywood. Hollywood is always ready to jump on the next great genius filmmaker and latch onto their success. Film festivals supply them with new talent. If you can get an agent on board prior to festival submittal then they can help you in positioning your film. The festivals are just as political as the studios. The best films don't necessarily make it into the best festivals. Contacts, politics, power, in addition to the subjective nature of films, are all part of festival acceptance or rejection. You can't take rejection personally. One critic will love your film and the next will hate it. Some festivals will only take world premieres. The larger festivals may not give you much press or a decent film slot in their line-up. You can get lost in the crowd, but you still have to enter the large festivals like Sundance, Cannes, Berlin, Venice, Toronto, etc. You have to determine what you want out of a festival. Does your film fit into the type of films normally shown at a certain festival? Do your research. If your film is denied acceptance at one festival does it hurt your chances for others? It is a possibility. The film industry is joined at the hip, so getting shut out of one festival may mean getting shut out of others. Of course, getting into one festival also means getting into other festivals. If you don't get into a festival, don't badmouth anyone in the tight connected industry because it will get around. Treat people with respect and you will get respect back...most of the time. If you don't get respect back then it's their loss and their problem. You are a much better person. Don't play down to anyone's level.

Film Markets

Markets are another means of selling your film. If you haven't gotten into the festivals then markets are another means for meeting distributors? You can pursue distributors on your own. Also, check out sales agents that represent films at those markets. Don't simply sign with a sales agent to rep your film. Do your research before signing with anyone.

Screen It Yourself

Yes, that's right! Rent a theater or ballroom or stage theater, rent a screen, rent a digital projector, sell the tickets, popcorn and soda and show it yourself. Many stage theaters are only used on weekends and they might be open to making a few extra dollars by hosting your film.

Plus, it brings more people to their theater, thus providing additional marketing for their plays and shows. Invite the press and give them free tickets. Invite agents, managers, etc. Make money by renting a place that is accessible to the general public. They will pay to see your film and you may be able to make back your costs and more.

CHAPTER **36**

The Golden Question

What else do you have? That is the golden question. People in the film industry that see your film and like what they see are always going to ask what other film ideas/scripts you have? You need to have several projects in development at all times. It's best to have two or three feature length scripts or ideas, sit-coms, web series, etc. that are well fleshed out so you can move on to the next project when someone wants to back you with money or support. Always be ready for the golden question, because you will be asked. Realize that with each film you make, it becomes your latest and greatest calling card. If you continue to improve and make better films then your chances of getting noticed improve every day. Keep improving. Keep moving forward. Keep moving up the Hollywood food chain with every film you make. There are no limits to what you can accomplish.

Conclusion

Filmmaking depends on how you use the technology available to you in order to tell your story. In the end it's all about you believing in yourself and taking action to make your films for the audience. You have to determine whether you want to make a blockbuster that grosses $500 million at the box office or a smaller character driven film that may only gross $50,000 at your local box office. This book was developed to give you what you need in order to be a filmmaker. Now it's all up to you. You have to choose whether you want to make films or make excuses. Most people will make excuses. I know you will make films. Your audience can't wait to see your films. Give them everything you've got. If you do that, you will be a success!

Keep in contact with me and feel free to ask me questions and give me updates on your progress. Good luck and don't forget to invite me to your premiere!

Best wishes for your success!
Curtis Kessinger

About the Author

Curtis Kessinger is an independent filmmaker living in Los Angeles. His career in the entertainment industry began as a professional stand-up comic, improv actor, and voiceover artist. He soon turned his attention to screenwriting and also launched the Malcolm Vincent Screenwriting Competition, which provided scripts to major film studios including Disney, Twentieth Century Fox and United Artists. He has worked almost every possible film job known to mankind. He has written, produced and directed two independent films and always has something in development. Curtis holds a BS in Mechanical Engineering (Southern Illinois University), a MBA (Pepperdine University), and has studied filmmaking at several universities as well as taught filmmaking. Curtis lives with his wife, children, cats and dogs...all of whom get coerced into working on his film shoots. Curtis loves to cast his films with real everyday people as well as seasoned professionals, so introduce yourself and get ready for your close up.

Glossary

Above-the-line: Costs associated with the film before production starts. The script/screenwriter, director, stars, etc.

Assistant Director: The right hand of the director. They assist the director and may fill in on certain tasks. They handle everything else, thus allowing the director to work with the performances of the cast.

Below-the-line: Costs associated with the actual production of the film...costs to make it.

Associate Producer: Anybody and everybody. These credits are handed out like candy on Halloween.

Best Boy: Best Boys are assistants to the Key Grip and Gaffer.

Boom Operator: Handles the mic usually on the boom pole.

Camera Operator: Physically operates the camera. That was an easy one to figure out.

Casting Director: They bring in the actors to read for your film.

Craft Services: The most important people...the food providers.

Development Deal: This is what everyone wants...to get paid to write a script based on an idea, rather than a finished script. A deal could be written to look at all future scripts/ideas you have. The deal is based on an idea that was pitched/presented to someone willing to buy the idea. The deal usually covers several drafts or more, but you could be one-and-done if the first draft is not up to their vision of the script.

Director: They work with the cast and everyone else to bring the script to life. It is their vision. They are number one...except for maybe the producer. This all depends on the credentials of the director.

Director of Photography (DP): They are also called the Cinematographer. They are in charge of camera. They may handle the camera or be telling a camera operator what to do.

Editor: Edits the film. They should be involved up front during pre-production to make sure they get what they need to edit.

Gaffer: The chief electrician and in charge of the electrical department. They are in charge of the lights and lighting crew. They work with the DP and director to get the lighting look they want for each shot. They will only work with the lights.

Green Light: Green light means the film is a go. Everything is ready to go...cast, crew and budget. It's a go! Throttle up. The studio is going to make the film. Of course the light can change to yellow and then red so don't put the down payment on that Beverly Hills Mansion just yet.

Grip: Build the camera supports such as cranes, dollies and the tracks they run on. They move cameras, sets, equipment, and maintain equipment on the set. They will usually work with anything other than the lights.

High Concept: In Hollywood terms this means a film/script is high concept if it can be told in one line...such as "A man has to save the earth from total destruction by a meteor!"

GLOSSARY

Key Grip: The chief grip. They are in charge of just about everything but lights. They handle the camera supports/mounts, light flags, cranes, etc.

Line Producer: Handles the daily on-the-set production and coordination for the film. They keep things on schedule and within budget...hopefully.

Makeup: They handle the makeup for the cast during production.

Overlap: Overlap of sound or dialog during shooting or in the finished film. Requires re-shooting/editing.

Pitching: Much like pitching a baseball, but instead you are pitching a story/script/film idea to a prospective buyer.

Points: It is a percentage of the sales profits of a film...including box office receipts, DVD sales, cable, etc. One point is equal to one percent. Net points means a percentage of the net sales receipts. Gross points means a percentage of the gross sales receipts. Gross points are what you want, but they are hard to get. If you are only getting net points then don't bet on ever receiving a dime. Net points refers to the points received after all costs are paid and all the other people in line ahead of you have received their piece of the pie. There will most likely not be any crumbs left for you.

Producer: The King. They hire everyone. They find the material, financing, director and make most decisions on cast and crew. They schedule, budget and manage the entire production from start to finish. They find the distributor for the film as well.

Production Assistant: Gopher this, gopher that! PA's are the people who do whatever is needed. Run to the store because they need more food. Run to the lab to get more raw film stock. They do all kinds of things.

Production Designer: Create the look of the film through their set design, costumes, etc. Also called Art Director.

Production Manager: They keep track of the expenses and make sure things are within budget. They may handle the line manager duties or work for them. Keep them happy.

Property Master: They handle and keep track of all the props.

Script Supervisor: This is one of the toughest jobs on the set. The supervisor keeps track of how each line was said...the actions...which lines were covered in which shot and take numbers. They keep continuity from shot to shot.

Second Unit: On larger budget films they are a separate group that shoots footage of less important things for the film. They will go out and shoot coverage shots of anything other than the main cast. They may shoot reaction shots of lesser cast members, but usually they shoot non-cast type coverage. There will be a director and DP for the second unit.

Shooting Script: This is a script with scene numbers in the margins of the script. The shooting script is used during production.

Sound Mixer: They are in charge of sound recording on the set.

Spec Script: A script written for free...meaning it was written hoping that it could be sold or produced. Speculating that it will be sold.

Turnaround: One of the most dreaded words in the Hollywood vocabulary. It means the script/project has been scrapped and is up for anyone to buy it. The owner doesn't want to produce it. If your script/film green light turns yellow then red your script/project will most likely be put into turnaround.

Additional Info and Resources

Software

There are software programs for every moviemaking aspect... screenwriting, budgeting, storyboarding, production scheduling, production design, costumes, contracts, editing, etc. All of these can save you precious time.

    www.artbunch.com - storyboards
    www.filmfestivals.com - film festival info
    www.script-o-rama.com - online scripts
    www.imsdb.com - online scripts
    www.joblo.com - online scripts
    www.dvinfo.net - DV filmmaker site
    www.dv.com - DV filmmaker site
    www.moviemaker.com - magazine for filmmakers
    www.filmtools.com - grip, electrical, lighting, sound and video supplies
    www.glidecam.com - camera supports for handheld shooting
    www.indiedolly.com - camera dollies
    www.ultracameramounts.com - camera mounts/equipment
    www.chimeralighting.com - lighting equipment
    www.arri.com - lighting equipment
    www.kinoflo.com - lighting equipment

www.lee.co.uk - lighting equipment
www.lowel.com - lighting equipment
www.bhphotovideo.com - cameras, lighting, etc.
www.ezfx.com - camera jibs
www.filmtvcontracts.com - contracts
www.dvxuser.com - filmmaker community
www.dga.org - Directors Guild
www.wga.org - Writers Guild
www.sag.org - Screen Actors Guild
www.sundance.org - Sundance site
www.sekonic.com - light meters
www.denecke.com - slates, audio accessories
www.dsclabs.com – chip charts, camera alignment charts
www.kodak.com - film, education
www.fotokem.com - lab, telecine
www.coffeysound.com -sound equipment
www.sennheiser.com - microphones, sound equipment
www.rycote.com - sound equipment
www.morguefile.com - photos for use
www.kickstarter.com - crowd funding/financing

www.ingramcontent.com/pod-product-compliance
Lightning Source LLC
Chambersburg PA
CBHW070737160426
43192CB00009B/1469